Labor Union Monopoly

Labor Union Monopoly

A Clear and Present Danger

by

Donald R. Richberg

HENRY REGNERY COMPANY

Chicago, 1957

Second printing

Foreword

AMERICANS ARE more out-of-date and ill-informed concerning the realities of the labor movement in the United States than they are in any other area of public interest. Fifty years ago, the picture of a labor union as a weak, idealistic organization of downtrodden workers struggling against an oppressive concentration of property power was often accurate. Any such picture of an established union today is not merely ridiculous; it is willfully or ignorantly untruthful.

Today the greatest concentrations of political and economic power in the United States of America are found—not in the over-regulated, over-criticized, over-investigated, and over-taxed business corporations—and certainly not in their hag-ridden, browbeaten, publicity-fearful managers. The greatest concentrations of political and economic power are found in the under-regulated, under-criticized, under-investigated, tax-exempt, and specially privileged labor organizations—and in their belligerent, aggressive, and far-too-often lawless and corrupt managers.

During the last quarter-century, while the American people kept vigilant guard against the formation of business monopolies, numerous labor union monopolies have been established behind their backs. These new and hidden monopolies—of which the public, bemused by carefully fostered misconceptions, remains blissfully unaware—carry with them all the dangers of any monopoly: the tendency that unlimited power concentrated in few hands will be used irresponsibly for personal or collective aggrandizement rather than for the common interest; the ease with which that power can, by direct or indirect pressures, bypass the established rules of law and order; the extreme difficulty of correcting concentrated power when it has grown corrupt.

Yet labor union monopoly also carries with it a threat unknown to other types of economic concentration, a threat that is contained in the long-range goals of the big labor leaders who decide to what uses their recently acquired power shall be put. Long ago, William Z. Foster, head of the American communists, wrote, "American society is headed to communism through an intermediary state of socialism which would be operated on the basis of a planned economy." The outstanding advocates and promoters of a planned economy today are the monopolistic, politically powerful leaders of organized labor.

Instead of being a movement of workers banded together for the protection and advancement of their legitimate interests in a free economy, the labor movement has now become a political movement with the objective of establishing a socialist labor government in control of the economic and social life of the nation. In part this transformation has been deliberate, through the counsels and strategy of those who were first of all political reformers, and only secondarily representatives of the laboring classes. But in the main it has happened because sincere labor leaders have become convinced that only through political power —the control of law making and enforcement—can they achieve the long-standing and legitimate goals of the labor movement. Unfortunately, the sincerity and good intentions of some of the builders of labor monopoly do not lessen the dangers of the power complex they have helped to establish.

Without an understanding of the historical processes through which labor monopoly has come about,

vii

one cannot appreciate the extent of the threat it poses. Accordingly, the first part of this book is largely the story of the political progress of labor unions in their influence over legislative, executive, and judicial officials. It is not a dull story of legislative drafting, law administration, and law interpretation, but a stimulating narrative of the behind-the-scenes political efforts which resulted in laws being written by favoring legislators, administered by favoring officials, and finally interpreted by favoring judges. The second part of the book shows how the fully developed labor monopolies operate today—as powers engaged in a legalized civil war endangering the basic structure of American economy and government. The danger is real, but not without remedy. The final chapters suggest what steps we can take to meet this "clear and present danger."

It was the fortune of the present author to render services for many years to many labor organizations, particularly from 1920 to 1933. During those years the foundations were laid, in law and in the coincident development of big business and big labor organizations, for the enormous growth of labor in numbers and power that began in the first administration of Franklin D. Roosevelt. After a service of

viii

two years in that administration, the author continued in private practice to render sporadic services in
the labor movement until as recently as 1943, by
which time the conflicting demands of a law practice
in representation of many corporate interests made
any further partisan representation of labor unions
impossible. Until recent years, however, he definitely
avoided any partisan representation of employer interests.

Thus it is fair to say that although the author is
severely critical of abuses of labor power and the excessive political ambitions of some labor leaders, he
has never been an antagonist of labor organizations
or labor leadership as such. He has never lost his
early faith and interest in unionism, and he still believes, as he did thirty years ago, that adequate organization and partisan representation of employee
interests is essential to the maintenance of a free economy. He still believes, as he did then, in the self-organization of labor and the maintenance of its interests
by collective bargaining. It should also be stated that
he was one of the earliest strong advocates of labor's
striving for and exercising the political power necessary to prevent hostile legislation and to secure a
fair and unbiased development of legal protections

of the natural rights of the worker. In writing this book, he feels that he still speaks for the legitimate interests of his friends in the labor movement—who, perhaps even as much as the general public, are endangered by the growth of labor monopoly.

DONALD R. RICHBERG

Contents

Labor Union Monopoly

PART 1

Labor Union Monopoly

PART 1

The Emergence of
Labor Union Monopolies

1

The Beginnings: The Railway Unions and Government Power

IT WOULD be impossible to tell in one readable volume the full story of how labor organizations have amassed economic and political power during the last twenty years. Small unions have grown to enormous size; a huge new federation has developed; and now the old American Federation of Labor and its late rival, the Congress of Industrial Organizations, are merged. There have been thousands of strikes, both large and comparatively small—some of them of great importance. There have been political campaigns, both local and national, in which labor has played a role, with great effect on local and national politics.

Yet the most significant development in the labor movement does not lie in its organizational growth, its conduct of strikes, or its participation in political

3

campaigns. The most significant development during the past twenty years has been a radical transformation of labor's basic goal. The leaders of the movement have always proclaimed, and still do, that their primary objective is the acquisition of sufficient economic power to protect the legitimate interests of the workers. Actually, their primary objective has become the acquisition of political power.

The beginnings of this shift in emphasis go back to World War I and the years immediately following. The early years of the twentieth century were for labor organizations largely a period of employer repression, legal restraint, and economic discouragement, with political power used more often against labor than for its benefit. Practically the only federal legislation sought and successfully won by labor was a provision in the Clayton Anti-trust Act of 1914 specifically declaring labor unions were not to be held conspiracies in restraint of trade. It is noteworthy that labor in this provision did not seek the positive action of federal law to stimulate union growth, but negative action designed to protect unions from prosecution under the anti-trust laws. This exemption of unions from the anti-monopoly laws did little immediately to encourage monopolistic growth of labor unions; indeed, the hope that unions would thus be

4

made exempt from anti-trust prosecution proved for many years to be illusory. It was not until the government began promoting and protecting the expansion of union power that the full implications of labor's exemption under the Clayton Act became apparent.

This government aid came first in the Railway Labor Act of 1926, which grew out of the railway shopmen's strike of 1922, which in turn developed out of the relationship established between railway employers and employees and the federal government during the first World War. As soon as the United States entered the war, the American Federation of Labor under the strong leadership of Samuel Gompers adopted a policy of thorough-going cooperation with the federal government. Essentially the program agreed upon was for the government to recognize the right of labor organizations to be consulted and to speak for labor, and for the unions to accept the necessity of continuous production and the elimination of anything in the nature of strikes. The program of cooperation was outstandingly successful on the railroads, which were taken over by the government and run under the supreme guidance of the Secretary of the Treasury, William G. McAdoo. McAdoo's policy of encouraging increased organization of the employees was particularly effective among the non-

5

operating workers such as the railway shopmen, who on many railroads had had a hard time organizing their men and obtaining recognition for their unions.

Despite McAdoo's friendly attitude, wage increases, made necessary by a rise in the cost of living, were long overdue by the end of hostilities. Hoping to obtain peacetime adjustments of wages and working conditions which would compensate them for their sacrificial cooperation during the war, the railway unions insisted that control of the roads should be retained by the government, and became strong advocates of what was called the Plumb Plan for a tri-partite operation of the railroads under the joint control of representatives of employers, employees, and the government. However, President Wilson was determined to return the roads to private operation, and this was of course also desired by the railroad managements. Despite the evangelistic fervor with which Glenn Plumb advocated his plan throughout the country, and despite the vigorous backing which railway labor gave him, the odds were all against any such plunge into permanent government ownership.

In this climate of opinion, the Transportation Act of 1920, providing for the return of the railroads to private operation, was enacted by Congress; but in order to meet the heavy problems of readjustment of

6

railroad wages and working conditions, there was set up a Railroad Labor Board to hear and attempt to adjust all labor–management disputes. A tri-partite board composed of an equal number (three) of representatives of the public, the employers, and the employees, it was invested with authority to hear disputes and to hand down, but not enforce, opinions and recommendations. It was hoped that the deliberations and decisions of such a tri-partite body would result in recommendations of such fairness that the pressure of public opinion would make them acceptable to all the disputants.

The Railroad Labor Board did not fulfill the fond expectations of its creators. With the return of the roads to private operation, management on many of the railroads initiated an intensive drive to reduce the new-found strength of the labor unions, particularly among the non-operating employees. The older long-established railroad brotherhoods which dominated the operating field (engineers, firemen, conductors, and trainmen particularly) were so strongly entrenched that employer antagonism to them had to be kept within reasonable bounds. But there was a strong hope among many railroad managers that the national organizations of the non-operating employees could be disintegrated and, indeed, that col-

7

lective bargaining with them could be largely avoided. Typical of this attitude was the slogan openly adopted by the Pennsylvania Railroad under the leadership of General Atterbury, who announced his policy as being "make no contracts with labor unions."

The effect of these anti-union policies soon became evident in the operations of the Railroad Labor Board. Its early actions were definitely favorable to the employees, whose requests for increased wages were approved for all classes of workers and put into effect by the Board's Decision No. 2. With the arrival of the depression of 1921, however, the Board agreed with the demands from railroad management for a reduction in the very wages which had been only recently increased. After a severe struggle before the Board, with the employer and government representatives combining against labor, there was handed down Decision No. 147 reducing wages all along the line. The decision aroused great hostility among the employees toward the Board, but in view of depression conditions, the reductions were made effective by the railroads without precipitating violent employee opposition.

As the depression continued and railroad management demanded another lowering of wages, a differ-

8

ence of attitude toward the several labor organizations became manifest. The Board passed over any reduction affecting the operating employees, but proceeded to put in effect a second reduction of the wages of the non-operators. This apparent discrimination led in the spring of 1922 to such a rank-and-file protest among the non-operating employees that the efforts of their union officials to preserve a peaceful operation became difficult, if not impossible.

At the time, the present writer was serving as a principal legal adviser to the non-operating unions and representing all the railway organizations before the Interstate Commerce Commission in proceedings involving valuation of the railroads. So he was a participant in many conferences of the officers of the shopmen unions as they attempted to formulate policies and programs to meet the situation. It was quite evident that although the officials of the unions were practically unanimous in their desire to avoid a strike, they simply did not have the rank-and-file support to carry out such a policy. Time and again, they said to one another: "We've simply got to have a strike. The men aren't going to stand for this second cut."

The inability of the leaders to control their own men demonstrated that labor leaders are necessarily responsive to the opinions of their constituents in

9

unions wherein the control of policy eventually is in the hands of the employees themselves. Older well-established unions often, indeed customarily, develop internal politics whereby a strong leadership can control rank-and-file sentiment by a combination of organized persuasion and internal pressure. The non-operating unions, because of their rapid growth during the period of federal control, had thousands of undigested members who had not come to accept procedures of discipline and acquiescence in leadership judgment. They had seen many concessions granted to their unions under government management and were convinced that all they had to do was to strike in force in order to compel the private managements to give in to their demands. Unaware of their own internal weakness and lack of solidarity, they did not realize that a lengthy strike would mean the gradual disintegration of their organization and the complete loss of its financial and numerical strength.

So it happened that the first really nation-wide strike of railway employees began in July, 1922. It is probably fair to say that the strike was welcomed by a substantial percentage of railway managements, who felt that here was an opportunity to enfeeble and

10

destroy most of the unions with which they were particularly disinclined to deal.

A serious, indeed one might say fatal, blow was dealt to the hopes of the striking union officials when it became evident from the beginning that the operating employees were not going to regard themselves as bound to strike in concert with the non-operating employees. If the operating employees had struck, the resulting almost universal stoppage of rail service would have forced drastic action by the railroads with the aid of government to break the strike, and there would have been a possibility of partial union success through compromise. Since, however, the operating brotherhoods merely rendered financial and vocal support of the strikers, the railroads were able by curtailing and neglecting maintenance to keep operating without too much difficulty for some weeks; and the strikers were compelled to exhaust their slender resources in what became more and more plainly a losing strike.

An effort to bring about a settlement was made by Mr. Herbert Hoover, then Secretary of Commerce, but he was firmly, indeed rudely, rebuffed by the railroad presidents to whom he personally addressed his plea. There also arose the possibility of a settlement by compromise with a group of less antagonistic railroad managers headed by President Daniel Willard of the Baltimore and Ohio; but when it became apparent that these negotiations might succeed and cause a break in the solid front of management opposition, heavy pressure was brought to bear on the national administration to intervene drastically against the strikers. Despite the rebuffs which President Harding himself had received from the railroad managements, they were able to induce Attorney-General Daugherty to file a comprehensive injunction suit against the striking unions. Without notice, and without opportunity for the strikers to be heard, he obtained a sweeping injunction, the effect of which would have been to paralyze the entire striking activities of the unions and deprive them of all means of financial and other support.

At the time of the federal injunction, something like three hundred local injunctions were outstanding, issued throughout the country to restrain the the strikers from all forms of illegal conduct. Despite all the instructions issued by the national officers of the unions and their refusal to defend individuals and local groups who might be accused of violent tactics, there could be no doubt that there had been a good deal of violence (probably on both sides) in the clash

12

between the strikers and non-strikers and the railroad guards. As the national head of one of the unions explained to their lawyer, who was urging greater efforts to stop violent outbreaks, it had to be recognized that "a strike ain't no pink tea."

It was then not surprising that the Attorney-General was able to back up his judicial complaint with an enormous volume of affidavits from all parts of the country, telling of violence which had interfered with railroad operations. It was, however, singularly unfair and hypocritical to claim that a national injunction was necessary to prevent the continuance of violence, when there were some three hundred injunctions already outstanding, and promising efforts were being made which indicated an early end of the strike. Indeed, despite the baneful effects of the government law suit, the union leaders had the courage and judgment to continue their negotiations and to work out a settlement with a group of railroads long before the Daugherty injunction suit reached its final judgment.

After taking evidence in the government injunction suit for many months in many cities, the lawyers for the unions advised their clients that there was so much evidence of widespread violence that the issuance of a permanent injunction could not be pre-

13

vented, even though any such injunction had become practically unnecessary. So, on the advice of counsel, the unions notified their lawyers to withdraw from the case and present no opposition to the entry of the final order which, though it might stigmatize their conduct in many ways unjustifiably, would be of no practical ill-effect.

The shopmen's strike taught the railway employees and their union leaders the futility of striking heavily against the public interest. They learned in the hard way that the heavier blow they delivered, the heavier would be the retaliation which they received. A strike injurious to limited private interests will not arouse much public indignation or turn effectively the forces of the law against the strikers. But when a strike hits a public service or some instrument of production or distribution of widespread public necessity, the more effective the strike becomes, the greater becomes the power of the forces aroused in opposition. It was not difficult after the shopmen's strike for impartial advisers among lawyers and politicians to get union leaders to agree that there must be devised some means of settling railway labor disputes which would give practical assurance of avoiding strikes. It had become evident that if management opposition was so strong or labor demands so unreasonable that a union was forced to choose between accepting a setback or striking, the odds would be all in favor of the union's defeat. The unions of the shop craft employees had been severely injured in every way by the strike. Their treasuries were depleted; one union that had started the strike with several million in its treasury ended half a million in debt. All the unions had lost enormously in membership. The unions had been particularly angered by the fact that a majority of the Railroad Labor Board had encouraged railroad employees to withdraw from their unions and continue to work, on the ground that the strike was in practical defiance of the government and, therefore, fundamentally wrong. Because of this action and the previous destructive rulings of the Board, the unions were determined on one goal above all others—to get rid of the Board. Recognizing, however, that they had to provide some substitute for a government machinery designed to prevent strikes, they realized that they could destroy the Board only if they developed a better anti-strike mechanism in its place. Their determination to do so was a fateful one. It necessitated a course of political action which involved repeal of the Transportation Act of 1920, the formulation of

15

a federal law to supplant it, and a program of successful lobbying to persuade Congress to carry out their desires.

The exigencies of World War I had involved the railway unions and the federal government in an intimate relationship which, during and immediately following the war, the unions had learned could be extremely beneficial to them. When, however, the depression of 1921 brought governmental action that was detrimental to the unions, they learned that federal power, especially when a great public interest was involved, was a two-edged sword that could be turned either against labor's enemies or against labor itself. An attempt by labor to control the use of the sword was implied. Though it was hardly realized at the time, the decision of the railway unions to attempt modification of the federal transportation law was a step toward labor control of governmental power.

2

The Fight for the Railway Labor Act

THE FIGHT for the Railway Labor Act, which was inaugurated in 1923, was one of the most critical battles over labor legislation ever waged in Congress. At the time such fundamental questions as the right of labor to organize, to be recognized by management, to engage in collective bargaining, and to establish trade agreements binding throughout a trade or industry were all bitterly in dispute. The country had just experienced the first and only nation-wide strike of railroad employees, and tremendous public antagonism and much fear of any increased power in organized labor had been aroused. The American people were just coming out of the first post-war depression and in no mood to be tolerant of labor disputes which interrupted production or distribution. Indeed, the strongest argument which the railroad employees had

17

was that they were voluntarily making proposals designed for the unusual purpose of preventing, rather than abetting, strikes.

In view of the climate of opinion, the leaders of the railway unions wisely turned back to previous experiments in the peaceful settlement of labor disputes and instructed their lawyers to work out a new law which would rely on processes of government mediation and voluntary arbitration. The lawyer to whom this task was particularly given was the present writer, and he delegated a part of the work to David E. Lilienthal, a brilliant young lawyer just out of Harvard who had come into his office in the summer of 1923. There were also consultations with lawyers representing individual unions—men such as Frank L. Mulholland of Toledo (representing the machinists) and James S. Easby-Smith of Washington, D.C. (representing the electrical workers), both of whom had joined with Richberg and his assistant, Leo J. Hassenauer, in fighting the Daugherty injunction suit. Hence, although the major part of the work in drafting and obtaining the passage of what became in 1926 the Railway Labor Act was carried on by Richberg, he will refer to this work as that done by "the lawyers."

In justice to the lawyers, it must be stated that they

18

developed a far more comprehensive scheme of legislation than their clients had originally in mind. They really endeavored to produce the draft of a law which, if it did not actually prevent strikes, would go a long way toward making them unlikely. They expanded the old ideas of government mediation so as to make it virtually imperative that mediation should be resorted to and be given full opportunity to make itself felt before any strike took place.

It took something like a year of intensive effort to work out the drafting of a new law. The bill as finally written for submission to Congress embodied three major methods of settling disputes without strikes. First, it was provided that management and labor should both use every reasonable effort to settle disputes amicably, and in case of unsettled disputes either party could invoke the services of a Federal Board of Mediation. The Board itself could proffer its services without waiting for them to be requested. Mediation thus became in effect obligatory, since it was bound to be proposed, and neither party to the dispute could bear the onus of refusing.

Second, if the mediators failed to bring about an agreement, they were required as their final act to propose arbitration. Either side could reject, but if it did so, it would again have to accept the responsi-

19

bility for having refused. If both agreed, and after appointing separate representatives could not agree on one or two neutrals (the arbitration boards being either three or six), then the Board of Mediation would be empowered to appoint such public representatives. An elaborate machinery of arbitration was provided; and, most important of all, arbitration agreements would be filed in and enforced by the federal courts. The grounds on which any appeal from such arbitration awards could be prosecuted were severely limited, so as to prevent any review of the merits of the awards by another tribunal.

Third, in order to avoid the accumulation of grievances which often led to strikes, there was elaborate provision in the bill for adjustment boards to whom disagreements over the interpretation of contracts or the application of discipline must be submitted; and the decisions of these adjustment boards were made binding. Thus was established compulsory arbitration of established rules—the so-called grievance disputes which are responsible for as much ill-feeling and eventual striking as any form of disagreement between management and labor.

When the bill drafted by the lawyers had met the approval of the labor unions executives, the question arose as to its introduction in Congress. Since the bill of course abolished the still-existent Railroad Labor Board, it was bound to create serious controversy. Senator LaFollette, a staunch friend of the unions, advised that Senator Howell introduce the bill in the Senate and that Representative Barkley of Kentucky, ranking Democratic member of the Interstate Commerce Committee, sponsor the bill in the House. Senator LaFollette and Senator Howell were Republican members of the Senate Interstate Commerce Committee, and the intention was to avoid making the bill a partisan political issue. Representative Barkley accepted the sponsorship and fought for the bill so resolutely and effectively that when he subsequently decided to run for the Senate he obtained powerful aid from the labor unions in his successful campaign.

After its introduction in Congress in 1924, the Howell-Barkley Bill followed a stormy course. In the Senate, particularly through the efforts of Senator LaFollette, the bill was reported out favorably by the committee with a margin of one vote. In the House, since it was impossible to get the bill reported out by a hostile committee, advantage was taken of a comparatively new procedure by which signatures were obtained in sufficient numbers to bring the bill out on the floor for consideration by the entire House; and the majority which had been obtained stood firm under Barkley's shrewd guidance through twenty-four roll calls, forced by the filibustering tactics of the Republican leadership. Finally, at eleven o'clock at night, Representative Barkley, convinced that the patience of the House was nearly exhausted, moved an adjournment. His final speech was characteristic. He told of a man, who, when asked what his deceased father's last words were, replied: "He didn't have any—Mother was with him to the end."

The railway unions seemed beaten when the Congress closed without the sponsors of the bill being able to get it on hearing again in the House, and without its having reached the Senate floor despite the favorable Committee report. Actually, the unions had succeeded far beyond their expectations, for the railroad managements which had fought the bill with the aid of the Republican leadership were thoroughly convinced that in the next session of Congress some sort of bill was going to be enacted. Conferences between the railroad attorneys and supporters of the Howell-Barkley Bill prior to the next session of Congress produced finally an understanding that the managements would appoint a committee to sit down with a committee of the labor executives to see if they could not work out a compromise bill. Something had to be

22

done, and it was wise counsel in the railroads which persuaded the managements that they would do better to participate in the writing of a law than to have one written over their objections.

With the managements converted from an attitude of opposition to one of cooperation, the unions had thus been highly successful in pushing their drafted measure, despite all the discredit which had been attached to them because of the unfortunate strike of 1922. Explanation of this success lies in their technique of promoting the legislation they desired—a technique which has been very little improved upon in recent years by other unions, but which has been frequently and successfully imitated. The railway unions drew men into Washington from all over the country, to tramp the marble corridors and interview every Senator and every Representative, to explain the proposed legislation and to get his views, and, if possible, to obtain his assurances of support.

Fortunately, in 1924 the unions had a good cause. They had a very fair bill, well designed to alleviate most of the causes of strikes and to provide a machinery which would insure in the vast majority of cases a peaceful settlement. The bill had not been drawn by men possessed of any illusion about their own economic or political power. Realizing that they were fighting an uphill battle, they had to rely upon the justice of their cause and the reasonableness of their proposals.

The feature of the bill which had encountered most opposition was the enormous cost of the adjustment boards for the settlement of the grievance cases. These boards had to be large in numbers and personnel, since litigations of infinite variety between something over a million and a half employees and their employers would be involved. No cheap and simple machinery could be devised, but the huge cost of the boards was nevertheless a serious obstacle to favorable consideration of the bill. Accordingly, when the management and labor conferees went to work at reorganizing the bill, the first thing they had to do was to eliminate these public boards. In their place, the revised bill provided only for the voluntary establishment of adjustment boards by systems or groups of railroads. The bill was thus seriously weakened—so much so, that by 1934 it had become plain that adjustment boards must be established, and these were written into the law by amendment.

Another major objection of the railroad managements to the bill was the lack of any provision for further action in case mediation failed and one or both parties rejected arbitration. There seemed noth-

24

ing then ahead but a strike, and that was what everyone wanted to avoid. The remedy suggested by the railroad managements was to establish a fact-finding board to make recommendations for settlement, which, even though not enforceable directly, would align public sentiment against the party that refused to follow them. The unions were opposed to such a board. They felt that as long as another tribunal was provided in the law there would be a disinclination on the part of both parties to work out an agreement directly through mediation or by arbitration, and that more and more cases would then go to a fact-finding board. They were also skeptical of the results of such a compulsory arbitration, even though the recommendations could not be enforced. Finally, however, an agreement was reached that in any cases where a substantial interruption of interstate commerce was threatened, the President could establish an Emergency Board and durng its hearings and for thirty days thereafter neither party would change the conditions out of which the dispute arose.

After the bill had been revised along the lines indicated, it received the blessings of both the employers and employees of the railroad industry, and was ready for introduction and practically assured of passage by the Congress. In these circumstances, the Republican

25

leadership which had vigorously fought the Howell–Barkley Bill was more than anxious to accept responsibility and claim credit for the passage of a new Railway Labor Act. The chairmen of both Senate and House committees insisted upon their privilege to introduce the bill, and the controversial Howell-Barkley Bill of 1924 became the Watson–Parker Bill of 1926.

The unions, however, took a sly revenge upon the leadership which had opposed them when they were weak but supported them when they were strong. They had written into the bill that its official title would be the Railway Labor Act, and always refused to give it the personal advertisement of a "Watson–Parker Act." Those staunch fighters, Senator Howell and Representative Barkley, smothered their personal feelings and lined up strongly in favor of the new bill. It was enacted by both houses with enormous majorities, only thirteen votes against it in either house, the only fight waged on it being by a small minority of intransigent railroads, aided and abetted by the misguided National Manufacturers Association.

Passage of the Railway Labor Act of 1926 was an event of double significance in the story of labor's rise to political power. Labor, on its first attempt to utilize governmental power for its own positive benefit, had been spectacularly successful. Thus was set a strategic pattern which persists into our own day. During 1924-26, however, labor, while seeking federal power for its own benefit, also—in part because it had to—took into consideration the interests of management and the public. In later years, the unions would remember the strategy of 1926 but not its spirit. The Railway Labor Act marks at one and the same time the point at which labor's assumption of political power began and the point to which it must return if it is to use that power legitimately.

3

Labor Unions Become Political

THUS THE Shopmen's Strike of 1922 brought
forth the Railway Labor Act of 1926, and organized
labor for the first time turned to government—not for
protection or defense against oppression, as in the
Clayton Act of 1914, but for active aid in exerting its
economic strength. The significance of this move was
not overlooked or ignored by old-line unions. The
American Federation of Labor, reared in the Gompers anti-socialist tradition of avoiding political activities, strongly questioned the wisdom of the
proposed law and endorsed it only with reluctance.
The violent opposition of the National Association of
Manufacturers may have helped to remove some of
the labor prejudice created against the act by union
collaboration with a majority of the railroad executives!

28

It is not in defense but in explanation of the N.A.M. opposition to point out that the act, since it obtained for labor the political aid of a federal law upholding its right to organize and bargain collectively, did raise a serious question. Here was a law which obligated employers to deal with unions and strengthened the organizing powers of the unions. To the employers who then dominated the N.A.M., such a law not only seemed a challenge to their claimed right to refuse to recognize a union; it also opened up the prospect of more partisan pro-labor legislation to follow. Indeed the Wagner Act of 1935 was a not-long-delayed realization of these fears.

It was, therefore, not surprising that a minority of the railroads did not join the collaborating majority and deliberately flouted the law for some years. Finally, in a clear case of violation, they were forced to the defense of "unconstitutionality," which was decided against them in a landmark opinion by Chief Justice Hughes in 1930. In this case was laid the foundation for a long line of decisions upholding the federal power to regulate labor relations in interstate commerce. Later federal laws have gone far beyond the modest limits of the Railway Labor Act and covered not only those engaged in interstate commerce but even occupations which "affected" interstate commerce as remotely as washing windows in an office building.

Most important has been the development of labor-law administration going again way beyond the gentle functioning of the Railway Mediation Board, which has little power to decide anything. But the sweep of decisions of the National Labor Relations Board is so great as to have created a long line of opinions supporting volumes of decisions in a field of law both unique and highly important.

But, before examining the effects of the so-called Wagner Act, it is well to point out the significance in the growth of labor union power of another act— passed, by the way, like the Railway Labor Act, in a Republican administration. This fact is emphasized to make it clear before we proceed that the writer has no partisan interest in describing the development of the political favoritism that has enabled labor unions to grow in numbers and in strength and to resist any effective political checks on their increasing monopolistic powers.

It is an exact fact that the greatest stimulus to union expansion was given under Democratic administrations in the period from 1935 to 1945. It is also a fact that the only modification of political bias in favor of unionism came in 1947, through a Republican majority in Congress. It is also a fact that organized labor has had more influence in Democratic national councils, despite Southern dissents, than in Republican national councils. It is also true that a special responsibility can be laid on one man, who was a Democratic President; this will become plain as our story unfolds. But there has been such an obvious catering to labor support by both parties and by practically all candidates that the growth of a monstrous private monopoly cannot be made the entire responsibility of any one party.

In 1932, during a Republican administration, a long-smoldering demand for a curb on federal court injunctions against labor blossomed into the Norris-LaGuardia Act, the history of which has some importance. Ever since the "old" Supreme Court denatured the Clayton Act of 1914 by holding that it practically did no more than to restate what the law always had been, organized labor had been seeking some direct curb on the injunctive powers of the federal courts.

It was all right to proclaim the Clayton law a "charter of labor" because it held that labor was not a commodity, that a labor union was not necessarily a monopolistic organization in restraint of trade and was not subject to restraint for lawfully proceeding to

31

carry out its legitimate activities. But, strictly construed, this law didn't give labor unions the privilege of using terroristic violence to accomplish objects clearly in restraint of trade and to build up nation-wide monopolies by lawlessly carrying out illegitimate objects.

It required some more federal law and the liberal interpretation of a "new" Supreme Court to endow the labor unions with the priceless privilege of becoming monopolistic dictators of our national economy. The first step—a change in the federal law—came in 1932; and, as one of the draftsmen of the Norris-LaGuardia Act, the writer claims the right to exonerate himself and his fellow draftsmen from any intention to produce such wholesale immunization of wrongful conduct as has followed the judicial construction of that law.

Specifically, the object of the Act was to stop the issuance of sweeping injunctions, without notice and on inadequate evidence, for the obvious purpose of paralyzing a strike. Senator Norris, Chairman of the Senate Judiciary Committee, felt that labor was entitled to relief from such abuses of injunctive power. He asked Professors Frankfurter and Sayre of Harvard, Witte of Wisconsin, Herman Oliphant of Columbia, and Donald Richberg to serve as a drafting committee to prepare such an anti-injunction bill. The Committee labored intensively for several days and finally evolved a document which was much too wordy and complicated but which all were willing to approve. Its incoherence, which gave it a deceptively conservative sound, unfortunately enabled a later day Supreme Court, on which one of the drafters sat, to give it a most unseemly scope.

When Norris received and approved the bill, he had Richberg explain it to Representative LaGuardia, who had no hesitation in quickly approving a product with so much "authority" behind it. Both Houses of Congress were weary with continual hammering on injunction evils. They passed the bill, and it was duly approved by a depressed President and became a law. Nine years later the Supreme Court used this act as the basis for a holding that the Clayton Act immunity had now been extended to cover a whole new line of labor disputes. This holding may not have shocked the one co-draftsman who sat on the Court; but it certainly shocked at least one of those draftsmen who was not on the bench. He agreed with dissenting Justice Roberts who wrote: "I venture to say that no court has ever undertaken so radically to legislate where Congress has refused so to do." (U.S. *v.* Hutcheson, 312 U.S. 219, 245.)

In the foregoing case and several others the Supreme Court has used the Norris-LaGuardia Act to infuse new life into the moribund Clayton Act "charter of labor." Indeed, one might well say that the Clayton Act "charter" has not only been given a new life, but a much more vicious life than any intelligent member of Congress who voted for either act, intended or even imagined. Even the Supreme Court Justices seem a bit appalled at the Frankenstein monster they have helped to create. One of them, Justice Black, wrote pathetically (325 U.S. 797, 810) that Congress had apparently given unions power "to shift our society from a competitive to a monopolistic economy." But the desirability of this, he wrote, "is a question for the determination of Congress." A remorseful labor congressman might well say: "Et tu Brute?"

Naturally one of the main factors in this hyperbolic construction of the Norris–LaGuardia Act was the passage of the Wagner Act in 1935 and the sustaining of its nation-wide application by the "reformed" but not yet "remade" Supreme Court in 1937. It is now appropriate to examine briefly the genesis of that Act and the reason for its extraordinarily one-sided administration.

The inner collapse of the N.R.A. (with its pro-labor Section 7a) came about during 1934 and 1935 from causes which have been amply reviewed by the writer in his book entitled *The Rainbow*. But since he was the head of the N.R.A. during its expiring three months, he can take the liberty of reiterating here that big business, little business, and organized labor all contributed to the scuttling of N.R.A. Big business objected to government supervision; little business objected to what it thought was big-business control of government supervision; and organized labor, although benefitting enormously from government aid, demanded some favoritisms which were not granted.

When the Supreme Court rang down the curtain in June, 1935, the writer had one outstanding prophecy that he had made to the Steel Institute, in which he was a government associate. "You are undermining the N.R.A. because you think it is too helpful to labor. The one thing you are going to get when the N.R.A. is gone is a much worse labor law. You won't get any pro-business law; but you will get pro-labor law." This was in no way a threat, but a statement of fact based on the knowledge that labor was already plotting a stronger pro-labor law which the administration would favor, while businessmen were so divided in their views and so competitive that they

35

could not get together on any substitute legislation.

The writer was not, however, one of the final drafts-men of the Wagner Act, enacted shortly after the slay-ing of the N.R.A. During the early stages of this drafting, he sought in vain to have the principles of the Railway Labor Act accepted: to impose upon both employer and employees the responsibility to use reasonable efforts to settle all labor disputes with-out strikes, and to give government mediators a fair opportunity to bring disputants into a peaceful set-tlement. When it became apparent that the proposed law was going to be one-sided naked favoritism for labor—a helpful weapon in strife and no instrument of peace—this particular veteran of labor battles with-drew from this legislative war-mongering which mas-queraded as a program of peace. The Wagner Act established a strong labor protective list of "unfair practices" by employers; but it took no account of protecting employers from the equally obvious and harmful "unfair practices" of labor. It tied the em-ployers down against even advocating their side of labor disputes while granting a sweeping license to the unions. The enormous injury to a free economy which was engendered by the act became soon evi-dent when its administration was undertaken by a crew of zealots who openly admitted that they conceived their function to be to help organized labor turn collective bargaining into collective coercion and assume a dominant role in industry.

There can be no question that in the past employer opposition to unionism had gone to extremes. Particularly, judicial favoritism of employers made a labor resort to political aid seem a justifiable use of government power, in order to establish a fair balance between the conflicting economic powers of property owners and wage earners. The organization of great numbers of workers and the guarantee of their freedom to use united pressures seemed the logical way to counteract the overwhelming, and often oppressive, power of the managers of large properties. Unhappily, as in most reforms, the battle between extremists on both sides became so bitter that reasonable compromise proposals became impractical. Dominance of one power by the other, rather than a balance between them became the goal.

Over this labor situation there presided a cheerful, but quietly embittered, man in the White House, who had begun his administration with what he regarded as a determined effort to save a free enterprise system of industry from destroying itself through its own blind disregard of social responsibilities. He had obtained an early cooperation from desperate, frightened businessmen. But as their panic subsided, they had inclined more and more to resent aid from Washington. They particularly resented the way in which Roosevelt had managed to enlist the cooperation of labor by encouraging and protecting labor organization.

So a small gulf between the administration rapidly widened; and despite the spectacular achievements of N.R.A. in stimulating a business revival, antagonism grew between the White House and all the centers of big business operations. The part played by top industrialists in first discrediting and then invalidating the N.R.A. was the final hostility which incited the famous "horse and buggy" press conference. It also assured labor a sympathetic and partisan aid in the speedy enactment of a law not only to salvage from the wreck of the N.R.A. all its labor benefits, but to add an enormous aid never before extended to organized labor by the federal government. The President's popularity and control of Congress, combined with labor pressure, were sufficient to sweep aside all legislative opposition and insure the passage of a thoroughly partisan law to promote the growth of the trade unions.

The biased administration of the Wagner Act was in drastic contrast to the impartial administration of

38

the Railway Labor Act. Indeed, the National Labor Relations Board openly asserted its interpretation of its duties to be to aid and protect union labor in any conflict with employers, with little regard for the merits of a particular controversy. There is no use reviewing here the radical influences within the National Labor Relations Board, which have since been exposed to show the influence there of not only labor extremists but also labor politicians, including those so far Left as to be subsequently identified as active communists. The simplest demonstration of the aid rendered by the Wagner Act and its administration is given by the Department of Labor estimates of the increase of labor union membership—from 3,728,000 in 1935 to 10,489,000 in 1941, with a further increase during the World War to 14,796,000 in 1945.

It is appropriate here to call attention to the generation of the Congress of Industrial Organizations in 1936-38, which had the effect of not only rendering eligible for union membership millions of workers not previously classified as belonging to the A.F. of L. crafts, but also creating a terrific competition between the new C.I.O. and the older A.F. of L. The latter increased its membership from 3,623,000 in 1938 to 6,931,000 in 1945, while the C.I.O., starting practically from scratch in 1937, except for the adherence of John L. Lewis' United Mine Workers, was credited with acquiring 6,000,000 members by 1945. While the employers watched helplessly from the sidelines, the A.F. of L. and the C.I.O. ran a nip-and-tuck race to unionize industry, with the track cleared by a favoring government and a highly partisan administration of labor law.

One inevitable result of this vast expansion in labor union memberships was a great expansion in the ambitions of labor leaders. They became more and more determined to establish absolute control of wages and working conditions in the hands of their collective coercionists, as the possibility of their dictating the terms of labor contracts grew. This was, of course, not an unusual or surprising exhibit of human nature. Businessmen had for many years been increasing the size of their operations until they reached such a point of dominance in a particular industry that they aspired to monopolistic controls to spare themselves the rigors of competition. The labor leaders, who had to fight for many years for the mere right to exist, suddenly found themselves not only complete victors in that fight, but also in a position of dominance in the economic fields wherein they first had sought to bargain and persuade and now found it possible to bully and coerce. That they should bully

40

and coerce was perhaps only natural. That they had models to follow perhaps made their assumption of power easier. But that they should be able, even while they became the oppressors, to persuade the public that they remained the spokesmen for the oppressed was hardly short of incredible.

4

The Radical Influence of the C. I. O.

IT WOULD be difficult to overestimate the influence of the C.I.O. in driving the entire labor movement into more radical tactics. Inherently, industrial unions seeking to organize all workers would be more militant and socialistic than the older trade unions. The craft worker's sense of superiority kept him from becoming easily an advocate of the "dictatorship of the proletariat"; and, unlike the member of an industrial union, he might gain superior wages without forcing general wage increases, which, because they affect labor costs and the cost of living much more drastically, require stronger "social propaganda." The industrial unions, as they sought to organize all the workers of an industry, moved inevitably to industry-wide, instead of single employer, bargaining and became, as they succeeded, monopolists not of an occupation but of an industry. All these influences within industrial unions would make their leaders and members acutely conscious of the social controls which government could exercise so helpfully in their behalf. Hence they easily became advocates of political action to advance socialistic policies and programs.

Most important in the C.I.O. movement was the rapid emergence into leadership of labor politicians of the Left wing, ranging from such a Moscow-trained socialist as Walter Reuther to a subsequently confessed communist such as Lee Pressman. The rise of such socialist planners was for a time not clearly evident because of the early leadership of the C.I.O. by John L. Lewis, who brought into the fold his mine workers, who had been of course always an industrial union, although maintaining the conventional pattern of an A.F. of L. union.

John L. Lewis himself had always been a militant but essentially conservative unionist. He was often violent in expression and ruthless in action, particularly in maintaining dictatorial control of his union; but he was always open to negotiation and suggestions of compromise, for he recognized what he called, with a grin, "the higher expediencies."[It became obvious early in the C.I.O. movement that the communists

43

were moving in to organize and control the new unions to the fullest extent possible. When the writer protested privately to Lewis against permitting these radical marplots to entrench themselves in his new movement, he smilingly admitted they were trying to get in, but asserted his ability to checkmate and eventually purge them.

How completely mistaken Lewis was in the caliber and character of his opponents was dramatically illustrated in the way in which one "good will" conference, developed by the writer, was destroyed. A very large employer who was a client and friend of Richberg suggested the possibility of a meeting with Lewis to see whether an amicable foundation could not be laid for genuine, two-sided discussion and bargaining over labor relations. Richberg took the matter up with Lewis and arranged for a meeting at Richberg's home, regarding himself as acting in the capacity of a friend of both.

Unfortunately, but not unreasonably, Lewis regarded Richberg as the employer's lawyer—and so without any advance notice brought *his* lawyer, Lee Pressman, with him. Although this was years before Pressman was finally compelled to acknowledge his communism, he was even then regarded with heavy suspicion by all employers, and Richberg had himself protested to Lewis that Pressman was a very unrelaible and highly prejudicial adviser. The "good will" conference promptly became a very cool and formal affair, nobody making even a pretense of open, frank discussion of critical issues.

These communist influences grew so strong and became so notorious that eventually, to retain any respectability as unions interested in a free enterprise system, the C.I.O. had to purge the worst of its communist-dominated unions. Nevertheless the socialist philosophy which is fundamental to communism indoctrinated the entire C.I.O. movement to such an extent that the leadership of such an avowed socialist as Walter Reuther could be maintained. Of course, such leaders as Reuther can be very vigorous (and even sincere) in their hostility to international communism; but the depth of their socialist thinking and planning remains as apparent as before.

The service that John L. Lewis gave to the C.I.O. can hardly be overestimated, although eventually he became intolerant of its activities and withdrew both himself and his submissive mine workers. Before doing this, however, he had laid the groundwork for the development of one of the most powerful and monopolistic of all present day unions—the Steel Workers' Union. The story of how he did this is one of the

45

most interesting and revealing chapters in labor union history and deserves an "inside" recital.

It happened to be the destiny of the writer to bring together in amicable negotiations Myron C. Taylor, Chairman of the Board of U.S. Steel Corporation, and John L. Lewis, then head of the rapidly growing Steel Workers' Union. When news of this surprising collaboration became public, there was immediately printed a romantic, but apocryphal, explanation which obtained wide circulation. According to this story, Mr. and Mrs. Taylor were lunching in the Mayflower, and Mrs. Taylor expressed a desire to meet Lewis, who was lunching at another table. (One interesting but contradictory fact is that Lewis quite regularly lunched, particularly when alone, at the Carlton, only a block from his office. It was a hotel in which he or his union was reputed to have a proprietary interest.) The fabulous story reported that Lewis was brought over to the Taylor table, and after some conversation, he and Mr. Taylor adjourned to Mr. Taylor's rooms in the hotel and began a discussion which eventuated in an agreement between the Steel Corporation and the Mine Workers' Union.

The facts regarding how Taylor and Lewis were brought together are much more extensive and much less romantic. The writer made a memorandum of

46

them years ago in the interests of historical accuracy, and this seems to be an appropriate place to publish it:

"It appeared likely in December 1936 that Lewis would engineer a simultaneous strike of the mine workers and of the organizing steel workers on April 1, 1937. This would precipitate a very difficult national situation shortly after Roosevelt would begin his second term in the White House. As a volunteer friend of the President, I [Richberg] went to him and suggested that I would try to see whether I could not bring about some peaceful solution of the struggle to organize the steel workers. I had always opposed the anti-unionism of the steel companies, as well as objections of other large corporations to the self-organization of their employees. In fact, I thought that large employers would do well to encourage organization, not of dishonest 'company unions,' but of really independent but cooperative organizations of their employees. All I asked was the presidential blessing on my work, but no active assistance.

"At this time Ed Stettinius, a good friend of mine, was Chairman of the Finance Committee of the corporation and Myron C. Taylor was Chairman of the Board and Chief Executive Officer. Accordingly, I discussed the whole question with Stettinius and obtained the idea that it would be possible to bring

47

Taylor and Lewis together for discussions if Mr. Taylor could somehow obtain an advance understanding that the Lewis policies and programs would not be incompatible with his idea of how the corporation should be run and what would be satisfactory labor relations with a union.

"This seemed a large order, but I took the matter up with Lewis, explaining that I was not a representative of the Steel Corporation, but endeavoring to establish the possibility of a negotiation through which the organization of the steel workers might be effected without a strike. John and I had several talks about this, usually at luncheon, interspersed with talks which I had with Stettinius.

"It was at one such luncheon that Lewis asked me with a twinkle in his eye whether I thought the steel company executives would recognize the 'higher expediencies.' I answered that, if I understood what he meant, I thought that most of them were capable of rising above a declared 'principle' of anti-unionism to accept a union if they felt that would really be for the best interests of their companies.

"Without directly presenting Mr. Taylor's desire for some formula of underlying principles, I did suggest to Lewis the preparation of a New Year's Day statement in which he would outline the purposes of

48

his new C.I.O. organization in such a manner as to encourage a more friendly attitude on the part of employers. It seemed to me that if the C.I.O. unions could be held out as organizations opposed to using the strike weapon except as a last measure of defense against oppressive policies, instead of as a constant measure of aggression, it might inaugurate a new era of industrial relations. Thus, in contrast with the policies of many A.F. of L. organizations, they could establish the policy of cooperating as far as possible with employers and not merely fighting them.

"With John's encouragement I worked out a sort of statement which I thought might be made and obtained various suggestions of revision which would make it acceptable to him. In the course of these discussions we gradually eliminated the particular thought of a New Year's Day statement and came down to the real issue of finding some broad statement which, presented to Mr. Taylor, would encourage him to undertake personal negotiations with Lewis.

"When matters had reached this situation I was informed by Stettinius that Mr. Taylor, who had been kept in touch with our discussions, had decided now to take the matter over personally. As a result of this, my participation in subsequent preliminaries became less and less, because Mr. Taylor was the kind of man who preferred to play his cards close to his chest without revealing them any more than was necessary to his associates.

"Indeed, when the final statement was drafted, upon which I had worked so hard and which became the basis for the negotiations, I had difficulty in getting a copy. However, Mr. Taylor did eventually send me a copy, which I feel justified in printing since it represents the result of a very important negotiation in which I played an inconspicuous but rather vital part. In the course of this negotiation I may mention that the steel company officials and John L. Lewis separately offered to pay me a compensation, realizing the amount of time I was putting in on the matter. I explained in each instance that I could not serve as a helpful mediator if I were being paid by either side and explained to each party that I had definitely rejected any payment of compensation by the other.

Lewis-Taylor Formula

1-13-37

In order to secure to workers the right of free association and collective bargaining, neither employers nor labor organizations should be permitted to dictate to wage earners the form of their association, or to control them in exercising their right to associate with fellow workers and to act together in democratic fashion to promote their common interests.

The object of a labor organization is not to create strife, but to provide an agency for collective action by employees in their relations with employers that will furnish assurances of industrial peace, which can only be obtained by assurances of industrial justice. If employers of labor will meet this effort half way, will cease obstruction to the self-organization of their employees, and will candidly recognize the right of their self chosen representatives to negotiate terms and conditions of employment, we should be able to move into an era of good feeling in which the prosperity of all can be the common concern of all, to be advanced by fair dealing with each other.

No group is more concerned with maintaining contracts and insuring continuity of production than the great mass of wage earners to whom the making of a secure and decent livelihood is a daily problem and an ever present anxiety. Give this assurance to the American worker, give him a self-respecting confidence that his own representatives have a real voice in the councils of industry, and you will give to the American people the greatest possible assurance that industrial conflicts will not impede our national progress.

"There are many persons who may not regard my part in the unionization of the steel industry as a creditable achievement—not because of the way in which it was done, but because of the later results. But I would stoutly insist that the self-organization of labor is a necessity in maintaining the freedom of labor in modern industry.

"If the principles enunciated in the foregoing document could control labor relations they would insure a harmony of cooperation beneficial to employers, employees and the public. The objectives of those who attempt consistently to work out programs of voluntary cooperation and individual liberty, to supplant programs of compulsory cooperation and class domination, may be thwarted by abuses of power by newly developed masters of human affairs, but that does not mean that the objectives were wrong. It simply means that new battles against would-be master men must be undertaken in the age-old struggle for human freedom."

One of the reasons for a hostile reaction in industry to the announcement of the agreement of the Corporation to recognize and deal with the Lewis union was that Mr. Taylor had given no warning to his associates in the industry that he had any such project under way. The executives of other steel companies deeply resented the fact that the Corporation, the accustomed leader of the industry, had, without notice or opportunity to protest, practically changed the long standing anti-union policy of the industry. In defense of Mr. Taylor it might be said that he probably knew that great obstacles would be raised against his projected action if any hint of its possibility leaked into antagonistic industrial and financial quarters.

It may seem ironic that unionization of the steel industry started on such a peaceful, almost anti-strike, declaration of principles. The new C.I.O. labor organizations have been notoriously less peaceful, more militant, and more recklessly wanton in their use of the strike weapon than the older A.F. of L. unions.

Lewis had been sincere in hoping that the inducements, which he used to persuade Taylor to recognize the new union, would lead to the adoption of a constructive labor policy; and certainly, the Corporation went a long way to demonstrate its own good faith. But an arrangement such as the Lewis-Taylor formula, which depended upon the continuing good will and cooperation of two single men and their ability to control their respective organizations, was after all impracticable. Lewis soon found himself unable to work any longer with the radical elements that had become so powerful in the C.I.O. Although he became president of the C.I.O. in 1938 when it was renamed the Congress of Industrial Organizations (formed in 1935 as the Committee for Industrial Organization,

53

excommunicated by the A.F. of L. in 1936), he resigned the presidency in 1940, and the United Mine Workers disaffiliated in 1942. His departure left the Lewis-Taylor formula without even the semblance of a guarantee from labor's side. Industry-wide organization of the steel workers—the payment made by the companies for the formula—remained.

Philip Murray succeeded Lewis as president of the C.I.O., and the early antagonisms between the old and new federations generated such bitterness that it required the passage of years and the deaths of both Murray and William Green, president of the A.F. of L., before a merger could be brought about in 1954-55. In the meantime, the overlapping jurisdictions of the A.F. of L. and C.I.O. unions resulted in an intense competition for members which would have checked the rise of monopolistic powers, except for the enormous growth, simultaneously, of unions of almost unlimited jurisdiction in both camps. There were, for example, the Teamsters in the A.F. of L., which expanded to nearly 1,400,000 members, and the Auto Workers, C.I.O., which rose to over 1,400,000 members (despite the A.F. of L. trade unions, such as the Machinists, with over 850,000 members). Then there was the huge, undisputed Steel Workers, C.I.O., which declared a membership of 1,250,000. In a more competitive situation, there were the Clothing Workers, C.I.O., 385,000, and the Garment Workers, A.F. of L., totalling about 500,-000; and the Electrical Workers, A.F. of L., 625,000, and Electrical Workers, C.I.O., over 300,000.

These large unions tended more and more to establish and maintain industry-wide standards—thus increasing the spread of monopolistic powers previously exercised by comparatively few unions, of which the United Mine Workers had been an outstanding example. Significantly, during the Second World War all organized labor received more aid and gave less cooperation to the government than it had during the First.

5

Growth of Labor Power During and Following the Second World War

During the First World War, the federal government was able to work with a united labor movement, largely dominated by a conservative leader, Samuel Gompers. During the Second World War, circumstances were not so fortunate. Instead, there were two fiercely competitive national federations, each determined to gain every possible advantage over, or equal to, the other. Labor Department estimates credited the C.I.O. with 5,000,000 members and the A.F. of L. with 4,500,000. By the end of the war, the figures were 7,000,000 for the A.F. of L. and 6,000,000 for the C.I.O. Obviously both trade and industrial unions had been very busy fattening their membership with the aid of war and government pressures.

One principal device of organized labor throughout the Second World War was to establish the closed union shop wherever possible. Just before our entrance into the war, President Roosevelt, seeking to reactivate collective bargaining between the Mine Workers and the Steel Industries' "captive mines," felt compelled to say: "I tell you frankly that the Government of the United States will not order now, nor will Congress pass legislation ordering a so-called closed shop." Nevertheless the government practically capitulated to this demand.

During the war, there developed so many controversies threatening strikes over the closed shop that the National War Labor Board felt it necessary to work out a scheme called "maintenance of membership," according to which employees were obligated to remain members of unions during the effective periods of existing contracts. The practical effect was to assure the closed shop, but the individual worker was given at least an opportunity to withdraw from a union without losing his job. Significant of the widespread pressures of organized labor during the war to increase its monopoly powers through compulsive unionism was a demand by even the conservative railway unions for union shop agreements, clearly prohibited by the Railway Labor Act. The Presidential emergency board to which the dispute was referred held the demand not only illegal but totally unnecessary to provide "union security" for these strongly entrenched organizations.

With the end of the war, two different elements of union activity attracted public attention and concern. First, the unions, stronger than ever, became more and more aggressive in the exercise of collective coercion. During the war, there had been over 13,000 strikes—a disgraceful record for "patriotic" labor. In 1946, the first year of peace, the unions made an all-time record of 5,000 strikes, involving 4,600,000 employees and resulting in 116,000,000 man-days idle. As Senator Taft pointed out in his speech to override Truman's veto of the Taft-Hartley Act, "[The American people] had been deluged with a series of strikes . . . strikes ordered for men who did not desire to strike . . . strikes against companies which had settled all differences with their own men . . . strikes in violation of collective bargaining agreements." There is no doubt that the overwhelming sentiment in Congress for a revision of the Wagner Act was generated in part by the exasperation with which a war-stricken people had watched the unions take advantage of war necessities to force unreasonable demands on private industry and government.

Another factor shaping public opinion was a realization of the extent of communist influence or actual control in far-too-many unions. During the war the fact that we were allied with Russia made public sentiment very susceptible to communist propaganda. But when the war ended and our erstwhile ally promptly began a cold war against us, American opinion began to boil up against the ruthless and highly political policies of communistically inclined unions.

Public concern about these two unsavory aspects of latter-day unionism was sufficiently great to support the passage by the Congress of the Taft–Hartley Act of 1947, even over President Truman's veto. Although the act was still infiltrated with labor union favoritism, its enactment improved labor relation law in mild degree. It was ridiculously labelled a "union busting law," but it provided only one substantial obstacle to labor monopolization—the provision that, although the act itself permitted union shop agreements, the state "right-to-work" laws were nevertheless to remain effective. As a result, the number of state right-to-work laws steadily increased, and union antagonism to these laws and to Taft-Hartley also became more bitter. The united efforts of the A.F. of L. and the C.I.O. to have these laws nullified by the Supreme Court ended in a unanimous upholding of their constitutionality in the year 1949.

Compulsory unionism remained so deeply resented

by public opinion that all the efforts of President Truman and other labor politicians in Congress and in the States to amend the Taft–Hartley Act and to nullify state right-to-work laws came to naught. The laws have not stopped the rise of labor union monopolies, but they have been a serious obstacle.

Before the passage of the Taft–Hartley Act, the subversive unions had been conspicuously present in the C.I.O.—the natural products of the early reckless policy of John L. Lewis; and the demand, both within and without the organization, for the C.I.O. to purge itself of communistically inclined leadership had grown in a few years to irresistible size. The non-communist-oath section of the act made it both imperative and comparatively easy for the C.I.O. in 1949-50 to expel eleven unions, including such pestiferous ones as the United Electrical Workers, Mine, Mill and Smelter Workers, Fur and Leather Workers, and International Longshoremen's Union. This was costly to the C.I.O. in loss of dues but helpful to its waning prestige; and it made possible the eventual merger with the A.F. of L.

The A.F. of L. itself had to undertake a long-neglected housecleaning to get rid of notoriously corrupt and racketeer unions, although the A.F. of L. had been able to preserve greater respectability with

60

all its corruptionists and extortionists than the C.I.O. with its odoriferous load of communist-led unions. The same difficulty is encountered in cleaning up vicious labor unions as is met in trying to clean up bad municipal governments. Too many businessmen will take the easier way of making terms with corruption and extortion rather than the hard way of fighting them with condemnation and exposure, which is promptly labelled anti-laborism. And many a courageous businessman who has started a fight has had to abandon it because of the apathy or ignorant antagonism of political and social leaders.

Despite the mild restraints of the Taft–Hartley Act and the state right-to-work laws, the unions steadily advanced their monopolistic powers during the post-war period. Total membership increased by about two million—a growth which may not seem impressive in comparison to that of the war years, but which was actually quite significant, since it meant greater economic power for unions already established in the major industries of the country.

The period also saw far more political action by labor leaders, who now attempted to wield an influence not merely over labor legislation, but generally in support of welfare statism. During the war, union officials learned how beneficial governmental favor-

61

itism could be; and they developed a very immediate and selfish interest in expanding government projects. According to federal law, whenever the government undertakes to do a job or to support a project, payment of "prevailing wages" must be insured. If these are determined by the Secretary of Labor, he is expected to establish union wages and see to it that private contractors maintain union conditions, even though in the locality of the project no such wages or conditions actually prevail. The enormous influence of the federal government in aiding the unions in all public-sponsored employments is enough reason to turn the most conservative labor official (if any such remain) into an ardent, though covert, socialist, who can advocate a "welfare state" and at the same time maintain the pretense that he is a staunch friend of free, private enterprise.

Up through 1945, all the major industries of the country were engaged primarily in meeting war needs, and the long arm of government reached into all large private businesses. To twist that powerful arm constantly to support union policies was the price union officials demanded for their "cooperation" in maintaining continuous, even though costly, production. Naturally, when the war was ended, the continued cooperation between federal politicians and labor leaders seemed desirable to both. The socialized state of war time, they felt, should now be succeeded by the socialized peacetime state, to the mutual advantage of both labor bosses and political bosses.

The Truman administration soon exhibited the favoritism toward labor that was to characterize it throughout—an early, striking example of which was Truman's radio address of October 30, 1945, asserting that industry as a whole could afford substantial wage increases without raising prices. The partisan support of labor by the administration was so consistent that a return of favors was in order. It was natural, though unprecedented, that most of the union officials took a strong stand for the Democrats in the national campaign of 1952.

The chief obstacle to this drive for political power by the labor bosses, directly in the Democratic party and indirectly in the government itself, was the disinclination of the rank and file to follow the political "advice" of labor leaders. To increase disciplinary control over this rank and file, compulsory unionism seemed an ideal weapon.

As long as men could leave the union and still retain employment, there was a definite limit to what union officials could do to force men to support political and economic programs. The members could

63

simply ignore orders and "advice" and if pressed too hard could leave the union. But by means of a new device called the "union security" agreement, the union, meaning the labor hierarchy, gained the "security" of a cruel weapon to enforce its orders. Technically the "union security" agreement does not establish the closed shop, since men who are not members of the union can be hired; but since they must join the union in order to retain their jobs, the practical effects are the same. Protesting or uncooperative members can be threatened with expulsion; and if expelled, they are subject to discharge on demand of the union officials. As one union president frankly told a congressional committee, he wanted compulsory unionism, not only to force non-members to join, but also to compel old members to follow orders.

Thus in the period following the Second World War, the growth of labor union monopoly continued. The unions increased the percentage of membership control in most industries. They nailed down closed shop contracts tighter than ever in such strongholds of the union closed shop as the printing and building trades, and resorted to the "union security" device where the closed shop could not be established. They gathered more and more strength from government favoritism, at least until 1953—and they did not lose ground notably after 1953 even though they were not always unduly favored.

It is simply inevitable that as long as unions gain numbers and disciplinary strength through compulsory unionism, which is practically if not legally effective, they will gain in the accumulation and exercise of monopolistic controls. Human nature being a fact and not a theory, organization managers who gain coercive powers will exercise them more and more, will rely less and less on merely persuasive inducements, and will become less and less responsive to cooperative appeals.

It must also be realized that an essential element of union monopoly power is its supplementary power to unleash mass violence in its support. The unwritten privilege of unions to ignore anti-crime laws has played a large part in developing and maintaining their arbitrary controls over a theoretically free economy. This use of strikes and lawless violence deserves, and will receive, separate consideration in one of the following chapters.

6

The Rail Unions: An Example of the Growth of Labor Monopoly Power

THE DANGERS of labor monopoly power, described generally in the preceding chapter, can perhaps be seen more clearly in the post-war development of one particular group of unions—those of the railway workers. For many years the four transportation brotherhoods represented a heavy majority of the engineers, firemen, conductors, and trainmen employed by the railroads; and their conservative use of their strength earned them the respect both of railroad managements and the public. After the passage of the Railway Labor Act in 1926, they proceeded in orderly fashion (as did the A.F. of L. rail unions) to gain increased wages and improved working conditions through negotiations and a considerable use of arbitrations. The railroad industry enjoyed twenty years of extraordinarily peaceful labor relations.

Naturally, it was a great shock to the country, and particularly to a "friendly" President, when the engineers and trainmen apparently lost their good sense and called a strike in 1946. It was obvious that the nation could not tolerate any long cessation of rail service. The President's indignant seizure of the railroads received such warm public support that the strike ended abruptly, with the unions accepting the President's terms. Here again was demonstrated the weakness of striking against the public interest, of having so much power over industry that it cannot be fully used without inviting damaging retaliation. The strength and weakness of the atomic bomb—and of poison gas, available, but not used in the Second World War—furnish analogies from the domain of war power.

It may be that realization of this weakness inherent in great monopoly power was in the minds of the rail unions when they launched in 1951 their campaign for compulsory unionism, and perhaps they did not seek an actual strengthening of bargaining power. At any rate, their Congressional witnesses testified that they had already all the bargaining power they needed. Indeed, they did have an overwhelming majority of workers of every class in the union memberships, and the law gave the unions with a majority class-membership the privilege of binding all minorities and individuals by their agreements. So perhaps the real objectives of their 1951 campaign were increased dues by the elimination of all "free riders"—that is, by conscripting all non-members—and increased discipline over all members already in the unions. ("You leave the union and you leave your job.")

Nevertheless, the effect of union shop agreements, previously illegal but legalized by the 1951 amendment to the law, was to force every worker in the railroads to join the appropriate union and become subject to the more or less united oligarchy of the labor union executives. It was the first time that Congress had ever in one law literally established a complete labor union monopoly of all employments in a major and most vital industry.

It may well be that Congressmen, remembering the quick settlement of the strike of 1946, blithely assumed that such a monopoly would be too powerful to be used against the public. There was obviously a menace to the whole country in putting it within the power of a few men (for not all the unions need act together) to paralyze transportation essential to the very life of the nation; Congress, apparently with an

optimistic hope that so devastating a weapon could
not be used, disregarded this menace.

The fact remained that a deadly power was put into
the hands of the rail union officials—a power to bulldoze, if not all the roads together, at least competitive
roads separately, with threats of a strike that would
mean disaster. The frightening power was demonstrated soon after the pro-monopoly amendment was
enacted. In 1952 the non-operating unions failed in
their first efforts to force a national negotiation of a
single sweeping union closed shop agreement. Then
a compliant President appointed a favoring Emergency Board which in due course recommended that
the railroad managements sign away the freedom of
all non-unionists.

By itself, economic coercion on a national scale
might still have failed, as it had in 1922 and 1946.
But before this combination of economic and political
power, individual roads and then sectional groups
gave way, and throughout the country union shop
agreements were signed. This left a few valiant railroads practically helpless against threats of strike and
unable to command any effective public support in
the battle. The naked monopoly power of the unions
was evident. No strike could be defeated because there
would be no one to run a railroad whose employees

stopped working. The temporary and permanent losses of even testing the effectiveness of such a strike would be intolerable.

Only one recourse was left to those still willing to battle against the complete monopolization of compulsory unionism. That was to deny the legal authority of the unions to make union shop agreements, on the ground that the 1951 amendment was unconstitutional. It had not yet been decided that it was within the power of Congress to deny to all the workers of an entire industry their constitutional right to work unless they surrendered their constitutional freedom of association. So the issue was presented to the courts in a large number of lawsuits—which at present writing are either pending or have been disposed of largely to the discouragement of those who have been fighting these last-ditch battles for the freedom of labor.

Regardless of whether there will be any relief to those still fighting to keep the wage earners free from oppression by their own champions—this much is certain: we have seen the spectacle of an entire industry subjected to the more and more arbitrary rule of a labor dictatorship which has established a legalized monopoly power over all employments in that industry. If the drive against state right-to-work laws and for nationally approved compulsory unionism succeeds, we shall see in one major industry after another the burgeoning of a similar labor dictatorship. Indeed, in such industries as steel, coal, and automobiles, the authority of a single union and its entrenched hierarchy is already much more menacing than the divided authority of the not always harmonious rail union heads.

The monopoly power of the rail unions may be too great to be used with utter recklessness in such a vital industry. But we have seen in the past that great harm can be done to the general welfare when steel, coal, or automobile production stops and remains stopped long enough to compel at least partial submission to unreasonable demands. The prospect of growing monopoly controls by labor, which make the only alternative to disaster the increase of prices to the public, is a most unhappy one. Increased wages, increased prices, inflation—increased wages, increased prices, inflation: as this vicious cycle continues, we shall face the absolute choice of either rocketing to ruin or else challenging the labor monopoly power that has been, and will be, so viciously abused in its selfish exploitation of our economy.

But it is not easy to challenge a power which has been built up with a legal favoritism and which has had the sanction of so many well-meaning but confused leaders of public opinion. The need is urgent for a re-education of teachers, preachers, editors, and columnists in the actual characteristics of intelligence, responsibility, and morality which prevail among the labor union autocracies of today. It is only by maintaining a public opinion based on ignorance and misrepresentation of their real character that such labor organizations are permitted to retain exemption from the restraints of anti-monopoly legislation and to increase year by year their monopolistic controls over the most vital industries of the nation.

7

The A. F. of L.— C. I. O. Merger

To UNDERSTAND the monopolistic conse-
quences of the A.F. of L. — C.I.O. merger, it is desirable at the outset to understand the true nature of
these federations and the limits of power which they
can and do exercise over the affiliated unions. Otherwise one may be inclined to exaggerate both the
powers and the responsibilities of the federations
themselves.

A federation of "autonomous" unions has a limited
power of discipline and practically no power to shape
the internal government of an affiliated union. For
example, neither the A.F. of L. nor the C.I.O. had or
have any control over the calling or conduct of a
strike. They have had and will have no control over
the election of officers or formulation or administration of policies of affiliated unions. They can lay down

certain standards of elementary morality and expel from affiliation unions which flagrantly disregard them—unions which are notoriously subversive or openly corrupt and operated for the sole benefit of racketeering bosses.

However, when it is noted that one of the largest A.F. of L. unions is dominated by men with extensive records as extortionists (see *Reader's Digest,* December, 1955) , and numerous other union officials have been repeatedly convicted of illegal practices, the big labor organizations will not be given great credit for the rare cases in which racketeer unions have been kept out or cast out of the fold.

The main use of federation is to provide the machinery for concerted action by unions which individually have the same purposes. The most evident area of common concern lies in the field of labor legislation and to a lesser extent in other political activities. The statement of "objects and principles" of the constitution of the merged federations, agreed on May 2, 1955, discloses another major interest, outside of legislation—the prevention of raiding by one union in another's domain. The first long step toward a merger was taken when a no-raiding agreement was signed December 16, 1953: "No union affiliated with either federation shall attempt to organize or to represent employees as to whom an established bargaining relationship exists between their employer and a union in the other federation." No-raiding, agreed upon as a desirable principle, has always proved difficult to carry out: it would relieve employers of some jurisdictional disputes and strikes, and at the same time end competitive disturbances of monopoly power.

Still another general object in merged federation is to establish permanently the status of each affiliated union as the only authentic union of a particular class or craft. Realization of this aim promises to eliminate a competitive element in labor organization, somewhat to the relief of employers, but with a tightening of industrial control exerted by all "recognized unions." In truth, it will shortly become impossible to organize any new union except in some field (if there is any) where no established organization has already staked out its domain. The difficulty of breaking into the territory occupied by existing unions has been recently demonstrated when a new organization attempted, against executive and judicial discouragement, to establish itself as a legally recognized union of railway employees. The cards are all stacked against such competition.

There are a lot of noble sentiments expressed in the

official "objects and principles" of the merged federations, but most of them boil down to an intent to expand and strengthen labor unions wherever concerted action to that end is possible. It is only fair, however, to give the hierarchies of A.F. of L. and C.I.O. credit for many good intentions. There is an explicit pledge "to protect the labor movement from any and all corrupt influences and from the undermining efforts of communist agencies." Nor should there be overlooked the intent "to give constructive aid in promoting the cause of peace and freedom in the world." Such "constructive aid" could be rendered right here in America if the new federation really undertook to cleanse the labor movement of all "corrupt influences," which are notoriously hostile to "peace and freedom"; but even the A.F. of L. action against the corrupt International Longshoremen's Association, although praiseworthy, was not supported but actually hindered by one most powerful A.F. of L. union.

At first glance, the A.F. of L. — C.I.O. merger seems to promise a combination of good and bad effects. As has been previously mentioned, there are many disadvantages to an employer in a competition between labor organizations to represent his employees. On the other hand, the elimination of all competition by such means as no-raiding agreements or union shop agreements means a tighter control over an employer (or over an entire industry) by a union monopoly. It is curious that a "no raiding" agreement between businessmen to eliminate competition for customers would be clearly an agreement "in restraint of trade." It may well be that management and labor can maintain better relations if the union vision of "no competition between workers" is realized; but it should then be accepted that a private monopoly power, here as elsewhere, cannot be safely tolerated except when restricted by public regulation. That restriction is, however, entirely unacceptable to union labor.

One feature of the A.F. of L. — C.I.O. merger definitely continues the concentration of labor power in few hands. Control of the new federation between conventions has been vested in an executive council of the president and secretary-treasurer plus twenty-seven vice-presidents. This means that, as heretofore, the heads of the strongest affiliated unions acting as vice-presidents will govern the federation. This is a very sensible arrangement to insure effective government; but it is also an arrangement which gives dominance in the federation to the heads of the larger unions—to 27 out of 153 union executives.

The total effect of the A.F. of L. — C.I.O. merger is

77

to increase the monopolistic powers of the individual affiliated unions. It reduces competition among themselves and provides a machinery for supplementing their separate coercive powers in economic "bargaining" and practical pressuring, by a concerted power of coercion, financing, voting, and propaganda that can become well-nigh irresistible.

8

Judicial Aid to Labor Union Monopolies

THE HISTORY of American labor unions, from
the end of the First World War up to the recent emergence of a single national labor federation, makes
plain how large a role government favoritism and
political action have played in promoting labor union
monopolies. The enactment of federal law is one part
of the story. First came the exemption of unions from
anti-monopoly laws in the Clayton Act of 1914, which
actually did little immediately to encourage monopolistic growth until the government began actively
promoting and protecting the expansion of union
power. This government aid was apparent in the
Railway Labor Act of 1926, which, however, as a
genuine peace program, justified to some extent
(prior to its amendment in 1951) its help to the

79

unions by its reciprocal protection of employers against strikes. Totally unjustified, on the other hand, was the violent labor partisanship of the Wagner Act of 1935, which was only slightly modified by the Taft-Hartley Act of 1947. Nor should we overlook the importance of the minimum wage and maximum hours laws which put a floor under but no ceiling over labor demands.

Even more significant than the enactment of law has been a sweeping line of decisions from the Supreme Court, which has contributed heavily to the expansion of labor union coercive powers. Three decisions and opinions inside a five-year period have supreme importance in demonstrating the Court's pro-labor monopoly influence.

First, in time, is the Apex Hosiery case (310 U.S. 469 [1940]) in which restraints of trade by organized violence were held by a majority of the Justices to be exempt from federal prosecution. A brief quotation from Chief Justice Hughes' indignant dissent will show how unnecessarily far the Court went in establishing this union privilege of lawlessness:

"When the Union demanded a closed shop agreement and, on its refusal, declared the strike, only eight of the Company's twenty-five hundred employees were members of the Union. The Company's plant was seized and held for several weeks. Its machinery and equipment were 'wantonly demolished or damaged to the extent of many thousands of dollars.'

"There was not merely a stoppage of production, but there was also a deliberate prevention of the shipment of finished goods to customers outside the State."

In answering the contention that the Clayton Act immunized this violation of the Sherman Act, Chief Justice Hughes noted that the Clayton Act only provided that the anti-trust laws should not be construed to forbid the existence and operation of labor organizations "or to forbid or restrain individual members of such organizations from *lawfully* carrying out the *legitimate* objects thereof; nor shall such organizations, or the members thereof, be held or construed to be illegal combinations or conspiracies in restraint of trade, under the anti-trust laws."

Then he commented: "The reference in the last clause to '*such* organizations' has manifest reference to what precedes, and the immunity conferred is only with respect to the 'lawfully carrying out' of their 'legitimate objects.'"

His final conclusion was: "Once it is decided, as this Court does decide, that the Sherman Act does not

81

except labor unions from its purview,—once it is decided, as this Court does decide, that the conduct here shown is not within the immunity conferred by the Clayton Act,—the Court, as it seems to me, has no option but to apply the Sherman Act in accordance with its express provisions."

The second case is U.S. *v.* Hutcheson (312 U.S. 219 [1941]), in which restraints of trade by strikes to enforce a secondary boycott were held not to be a conspiracy in violation of the Sherman Law. Here the opinion reversed the previous limited construction of the immunity conferred by the Clayton Act on the ground that the Norris-LaGuardia Act had expanded the Clayton Act immunity "by infusing into it the immunized trade union activities as redefined by the later Act."

Justice Roberts, dissenting, pointed out that it was improper for the Court to hold that "because Congress forbade the issuing of injunctions to restrain certain conduct it intended to repeal the provisions of the Sherman Act authorizing actions at law and criminal prosecutions for the commission of torts and crimes defined by the anti-trust laws." He denounced this as radical legislation by the Court "where Congress has refused to do so."

In the third case, Allen Bradley *v.* Local Union No. 3 (325 U.S. 797 [1945]), the Court reaped the full evil product of its previous rulings in finding itself, according to the majority, helpless to prevent baneful exercises of monopoly power by labor unions. The Court found that the Electrical Workers Union was establishing by agreements with employers a monopoly in the sale of electrical equipment in New York City: "It intended to and did restrain trade and monopolize the supply of electrical equipment in the New York City area to the exclusion of equipment manufactured in and shipped in from other states, and did also control its price and discriminate between its would-be customers."

So the Court says: "Our problem in this case is therefore a very narrow one—do labor unions violate the Sherman Act when, in order to further their own interests as wage earners, they aid and abet businessmen to do the precise things which that Act prohibits?"

The Court sagely observes that Congress did not intend to give labor unions the power to destroy a competitive economy, the opinion using this strong language: "Seldom, if ever, has it been claimed before, that by permitting labor unions to carry on their own activities, Congress intended completely to abdicate its constitutional power to regulate interstate commerce and to empower interested business groups to shift our society from a competitive to a monopolistic economy."

The Court goes on to acknowledge the inconsistency in a law which provides that labor unions alone can destroy competition but not in combination with business groups. The opinion observes: "This, it is argued, brings about a wholly undesirable result—one which leaves labor unions free to engage in conduct which restrains trade. But the desirability of such an exemption of labor unions is a question for the determination of Congress."

Thus we arrive at substantially the following situation. The Supreme Court, by highly debatable construction of the statutes, has arrived at the place where even the Court understands that the law it has laid down is incompatible with the preservation of a competitive economy, which is the necessary economic foundation for the political government established by the Constitution of the United States. In this dilemma, faced with the results of its own bad lawmaking, the Court advises an injured people to get the Congress to change the law!

Once more it seems appropriate to quote a dissenting Justice, to make it clear that the Court's action has been here fairly criticized. Justice Roberts wrote as follows: "Unless I misread the opinion, the union is at liberty to impose every term and condition as shown by the record in this case and to enforce those conditions and procure an agreement from each employer to such conditions by calling strikes, by lock-out, and boycott, provided only such employer agrees for himself alone and not in concert with any other. . . . The course of decision in this Court has now created a situation in which, by concerted action, unions may set up a wall around a municipality of millions of inhabitants against importation of any goods if the union is careful to make separate contracts with each employer, and if the union and employers are able to convince the Court that, while all employers have such agreements, each acted independently in making them—this notwithstanding the avowed purpose to exclude goods not made in that city by the members of the union; notwithstanding the fact that the purpose and inevitable result is the stifling of competition in interstate trade and the creation of a monopoly."

He concluded: "This Court, as a result of its past decisions, is in the predicament that whatever it decides must entail disastrous results."

The cases just reviewed and many of the same tenor

85

would have enough evil effect if they simply exempted unions from prosecution for monopolistic restraints of what is strictly interstate commerce. But the Supreme Court has steadily broadened the domain of federal authority to include within it any activity which even remotely "affects" interstate commerce— such as the work of service employees in a building only 58 per cent of whose rentable area was occupied by a company actually engaged in interstate commerce. (325 U.S. 697.) So instead of subjecting wrong-doing labor unions to prosecution for violation of both federal and state anti-monopoly laws, the Court has extended a federal exemption to cover practically any union activity of any substantial importance.

Furthermore, the general exemption of labor unions from a responsibility which would subject other organizations or individuals to public or private restraint makes the exercise of union monopoly powers particularly vicious. Consider for example the case of Hunt *v.* Crumboch, 325 U.S. 821. Here a union refused to permit members to work for one particular employer and refused to permit his employees to join the union. As a result, they completely destroyed his business, in revenge for his previous

86

hostility. The majority of the Supreme Court held such a conspiracy to punish an employer was a legitimate exercise of the unrestricted rights of concerted action with which labor organizations have been endowed by federal law. It is at least comforting to note that four Justices of the Supreme Court dissented, holding that the conspiracy was within the prohibition of the Sherman Act and not within any immunity conferred by the Clayton Act.

Mr. Justice Jackson, in one of the dissenting opinions, made the following trenchant observation: "With this decision, the labor movement has come full circle." After pointing out how the workers had struggled long for their freedom, he continued: "This Court now sustains the claim of a union to the right to deny participation in the economic world to an employer simply because the union dislikes him. This Court permits to employees the same arbitrary dominance over the economic sphere which they control that labor so long, so bitterly and so rightly asserted should belong to no man."

This very brief review of the aid rendered to the growth of union monopolies by judicial rulings should not be concluded without at least a reference to one extraordinarily bad decision about which a volume might (but will not) be written. The racketeering of so many unions in compelling needless work to be done, or employees hired, or duplicate work paid for, became so notorious and offensive that Congress was finally moved to pass an Anti-Racketeering Act. One of the most outrageous rackets was, and is, that of the Teamsters Union in requiring a union teamster to be hired to drive into New York City, even though he is not wanted and does no work.

When this practice finally came before the Supreme Court in 1942, in a conviction for violating the Act, the Court held that since payments were made for a "service" (even though unwanted and unused) they were not violations of the law—even though that sort of hold-up was exactly what the law was passed to prevent! As the indignant, dissenting Chief Justice wrote, this decision tended to make "common law robbery an innocent pastime."

Without extending this review to the length of boredom, it is hoped that enough has been written to lay a heavy responsibility on the Supreme Court for outdoing even Congress in unwarranted favoritism for labor unions. This favoritism has vested the union with privileges which have been abused to such a point that even the judicial creators have become obviously ashamed of their work. But there is little comfort in occasional expressions of contrition from a Court which continues year after year to treat labor unions as specially endowed with virtues—which must, apparently, also justify their endowment with special privileges to violate laws supposed to be enforced, without fear or favor, upon all citizens and organizations with equal vigor.

PART II

Labor Monopoly in Action

9

Strikes

UNION MONOPOLY controls over industry are made effective by the power of striking. The strike in itself is economic violence, and behind it is the threat and resort to physical violence. This is not always evident in small strikes or even in industry-wide strikes. But it is this threat of lawless force that gives potency to the lawful coercion of a so-called peaceful strike.

There would be little need of picketing, and certainly no reason for mass picketing, except for the purpose of forcibly preventing men from working. It has been well said that the right to strike does not mean simply the right to quit a job. In practical application it means the right to hold a job while not working at it, the right of the striker not only to stop

93

working but also to prevent anyone else from taking his job.

It is highly questionable whether any long strike could be won by labor without the use of lawless methods of preventing a replacement of strikers or a steady drift of strikers back to work. Nowadays, there is sure to be so much reasonableness in a large employer's efforts to prevent a strike, so much unreason in the ultimate labor demands, and so much individual hardship in striking, that a long strike would seldom be won if employees and would-be employees could peacefully accept offers of employment.

That is why the foul shape of terrorism is always lurking in the shadows behind even apparently peaceful strikes. If any real effort is made by an employer to operate and by willing workers to work despite a strike ban, then suddenly crude violence appears in support of the strike. Such violence is always hypocritically disavowed by strike leaders; but dynamiting, stench-bombing, train-wrecking, cable-cutting, window-smashing, and physical assaults and intimidation of would-be workers and their families do not happen by coincidence as spontaneous outbursts of individual action. Professional sluggers, imported from distant places, do not appear by chance on picket lines. Mass picketing, auto-smashing, and similar organized lawlessness must be conceded to be part and parcel of authorized strike activities. It would require several volumes to recount the stories of strike violence of even recent years. But, for the benefit of those gullible defenders of any and every union labor performance, it may be worth while to review briefly the experience of one company which has made a stubborn fight against a crippling strike. This company for over two years has been able to keep its plant going, despite the use of every variety of brutal violence which a powerful labor organization can employ to hamper the employer and intimidate his employees.

On April 5, 1954, the United Auto Workers Union, C.I.O., began a strike against the Kohler Company of Kohler, Wisconsin. This strike obviously could not be won by mere peaceful striking, since the average weekly earnings of Kohler employees were considerably higher than any comparable earnings (Kohler $87.45; entire industry $76.04) , and working conditions were notably superior. Nor can it be assumed that employees would voluntarily give up these good wages and conditions to force compulsory unionism on themselves or to compel the management to accept the varieties of union control over management which the union bosses were demanding.

That is why, from the day the strike started, the union threw mass picketing and other obstructions around the plant to prevent employees from going to work. For fifty-four days all production was prevented. Then, after an orgy of mass picketing, rioting, and widespread individual violence, the Wisconsin Employment Relations Board, having issued an order against the union to "cease and desist" from its unlawful activities, applied for an injunction to enforce its order. Whereupon the picket lines were reduced and employees in large numbers returned to their jobs.

In the hearings before the WERB, testimony showed that massed pickets had physically prevented employees from going to work from the first day of the strike, automobile access to the plant had been blocked, homes had been picketed and would-be workers threatened by night and day telephone calls, and individuals physically assaulted. It was also testified that when the sheriff was asked for protective escort into the plant, he had advised workers to go home and avoid bloodshed. It is not surprising that the sheriff was enthusiastically supported by the union for reelection in the fall.

When mass picketing was curbed, terrorism increased. Paint bombs were thrown at homes and automobiles; tires were slashed and paint remover splashed on cars; sugar and sand put in gasoline tanks; windows of homes smashed; and gardens ruined. One outrageous assault by a huge, imported goon sent a small worker to the hospital with a crushed chest, a pierced lung, and fractured ribs. This union "educator" was convicted, after a defense by the union attorney, and sentenced to one to two years in prison, whereupon the union acclaimed him as a martyr and denounced the judge who sentenced him. The judge had been so indiscreet as to remark in sentencing this thug that he was lucky that his victim had recovered so he was not being sentenced for murder!

The union attack on the judge went so far as to boycott food markets in which the judge had a financial interest. The union's hired criminal was eulogized in official publications. Yet unions always claim that they do not "condone" violence. It was made clear a hundred times in the Kohler strike that the entire effort to win the strike was based on the terrorizing of all would-be employees. It is a tribute to the amazing courage of scores of men and women that they persisted in their determination to earn a living in Kohler despite every kind of terroristic discouragement.

It is particularly interesting to note that in the

Kohler strike the union sought to gain the protective jurisdiction of the federal government and to block the administration of state law. On the familiar ground that federal law had occupied the field and that the Kohler Company was engaged in interstate commerce, a federal injunction against state action was sought. Since the federal courts are always insisting that violence and local crimes are subject to local punishment, this flight to a refuge in federal law would be humorous if it were not so dangerous. There would be no effective remedy in complaining to the National Labor Relations Board—only a long-drawn-out proceeding resulting in trifling relief "too little and too late."

On the other hand, the action of the State Board was reasonably prompt and effective to stop some clearly illegal practices. Fortunately, at the end of a long litigation the United States Supreme Court has upheld the authority of Wisconsin to protect its citizens from organized lawlessness and criminality.

Maintenance of the Kohler strike by organized crime and hired criminals is clearly a policy and program of the national C.I.O., being carried out by its top national officers. The common pretense that "local hot-heads" are responsible for physical assaults and terrorism cannot be used to whitewash either the

United Automobile Workers or the C.I.O. as national organizations.

The top officers of the UAW and the C.I.O., Walter Reuther and Emil Mazey, have taken a prominent part in the strike. The financial support of the strike goes far beyond any local ability. Squads of strong-armed thugs have been sent from Detroit to intimidate strikers as well as non-strikers and to carry on the rough stuff that will discourage both strikers and non-strikers from working for Kohler. The cynical practice of calling these criminals and muscle men "educators," who are sent as "experts to aid in collective bargaining," is a good example of the arrogance with which high officials in the huge monopoly unions sneer at the public opinion which is expected to support their lawless procedures.

The Kohler strike brought to public attention another type of law breaking—the arranging of secondary boycotts to prevent raw materials from coming in or finished goods from going out. When the C.I.O. managed by mob violence to close the port of Sheboygan to a vessel bringing clay to the Kohler Company, it aroused mild public interest. But when the large port of Milwaukee was closed to the same shipment by political and economic pressure, public attention was directed to the Kohler strike in a manner which

99

revealed the lengths to which the C.I.O. was ready to go to win this losing strike. Far away from Kohler some 50,000 Milwaukee unionists threatened a city-wide strike and thus prevented the unloading at the municipal docks.

It has seemed desirable to use the Kohler strike as an example of labor union violence because the record is so clearly written, the strike has been unusually long, and failure to win it has incited the union to utilize so many forms of lawlessness and the crudest methods of terrorism. To prevent any assumption that such tactics are exceptional whenever an employer resists a strike it is only necessary to recall attention to the newspaper accounts of a few other contemporary strikes. In a strike against the Louisville and Nashville Railroad there was dynamiting, train-wrecking, terrorism, and individual violence. In a strike against the Southern Telephone Company, cable-cutting, a job for experts, was one of the major weapons used. Extensive violence in the Perfect Circle strike was widely reported.

The *Reader's Digest* recently published a condensation of a *Saturday Evening Post* article detailing fifteen months of continuing violence when the Mine Workers attempted, in vain, to organize a mine at Widen, West Virginia. The reign of terror included the destruction by dynamite of three railroad bridges, two electric-power substations, and a high-tension tower. Automobiles were overturned, dynamited, or rocked. In an ambush, one man was killed and others wounded. All this was done to compel men to join a union, which plainly a majority of them did not want to join. Instigation of the so-called "strike" by the national union was phony from first to last; it was simply an effort to force unwilling workers to become unionists.

Organized violence, either active or held in reserve in every strike, makes it evident that a large percentage of unionized employees would not support a long strike, if their support were not compelled by the union officers who assume to represent them. It is easy to get a heavy vote originally approving a strike, since the workers are told that their representatives must have this weapon in their hands or else they cannot "bargain" successfully. Thereafter, antagonism is whipped up against the employer by every conceivable biased criticism, and every assurance given the men that if they stand firm they will quickly win.

When a strike is called, a war is proclaimed, with resort to all the propaganda devices used in wars with a national enemy. Desertion of the battle line brings retaliation and disgrace. If a strike is won, all loyalists will be protected; even if a strike is lost, disloyalists will suffer indefinitely from the hatred of their fellow workers who sacrificed in vain. It is not surprising that decent, law-abiding men and women, who would refuse to use the brutal methods of hired goons, will nevertheless participate in strike mobs. They have been induced to feel they are in a civil war. Their livelihood is at stake. Having thrown down the gage of battle, they must fight on until they win or lose all together. Thus it is not hard to understand why the rank and file of workers will support the union leaders in a vicious strike, and why the union bosses will stoop to violence and crime to win a desperate struggle.

There is only one way in which this weapon of strike violence can be denied to the labor monopolists who already have too much coercive power. That way is to enact state laws sternly forbidding all forms of intimidation and terrorism, and to select state officials willing to enforce the laws. This is not an easy remedy, because the political power of organized labor is frequently great enough to paralyze all three arms of government—the legislative, executive, and judicial. Nevertheless, there should be popular support of a rule of law even among the rank and file of unionists, who, like all citizens of the community, have an interest in the maintenance of order. If a strike cannot be won peacefully by labor monopolists who can shut down an entire industry or any single large plant, they should not have a second chance to win by civil warfare. The rule of law should extend to the formulation of labor demands. These would be modified in a healthy way if they were required to be sufficiently reasonable to have the hearty support of at least a large majority of those who are supposed to be benefitted by them.

10

Finances

ONE OF THE special advantages of a labor union monopoly lies in the great number of those supporting it, willingly or unwillingly. The advantages of overpowering number in stopping work by concerted action and of having a huge number of members susceptible to being voted in droves to support what is claimed to be their own personal—and financial—interests are obvious. Not so obvious but of great importance is the fact that a vast number of union members permits the raising of vast sums of money by means of small contributions.

The exact financial strength of unions as a whole or of individual unions cannot be easily calculated because so little is freely revealed. One large source of revenues—assessments, which are levied for a great variety of purposes and in varying amounts—is largely hidden. Nevertheless, enough information can be obtained from union constitutions and official reports regarding amounts of dues and numbers of declared memberships to make possible quite reliable estimates. Amounts of initiation fees and dues can be ascertained for a substantial percentage of the unions, and per capita taxes to the national union may show the probable amount of local dues collected. From such sources it has been carefully estimated that union revenues from dues alone probably exceed $450,000,-000 annually. What percentage of this vast total goes to support the concentrated power of the national unions and what is left or returned to the local unions, it would be difficult to compute; but in some individual cases the computation can be made.

One example of the use of union dues is provided by the United Automobile Workers, C.I.O. Ordinarily, the regular monthly dues are $2.50. Of this amount, $1.25 per person is paid to the central organization, which, from 1,400,000 members, thus receives usually a monthly income of $1,750,000. However, in April, 1955, the U.A.W.–C.I.O. increased regular local dues to $5.00 in order to raise a guaranteed-annual-wage strike-fund of $25,000,000. After the accomplishment of this project, dues were to be returned to $2.50, but if strike costs should reduce the fund below $20,000,000, then dues would be increased to $3.50 until $25,000,000 was again reached.

In such a scheme as this, one type of tactics of the union monopolists becomes clear and terrifying. Strikers against one great producer can be supported by increasing the dues of all the other workers. While the stricken producer is losing enormous amounts of money, his competitors will temporarily benefit, and even if competitors were willing to make common cause with the stricken company (imagine it!) they would be prosecuted as an illegal combination in restraint of trade. Thus the labor monopolist uses his power of numbers and money to coerce the businessman, who is forbidden to fight back with similar monopoly power. Who could resist?

Another use of union revenues can be seen in the operations of the Steel Workers Union, C.I.O., in which, by check-off, dues are paid by the employer to the national union, which takes its cut of $1.50 before remitting to the local unions their share, normally also a balance of $1.50 per member per month. In Steel we have had an example of the other type of tactics—a monopoly strike against an entire industry. Such a strike may be regarded as cunning, since the injury to the industry, the public generally, and the national defense will be so great that no steel strike can actually last long. Because its naked monopoly power is cruelly visible, the union is forced to make special efforts to throw the blame for a strike upon the great steel companies, which already start with the disadvantage of not being exceptionally popular. Of course, the union complains that these "oppressive monsters"—these "fat profiteering exploiters"—are not willing to bargain fairly: they make "niggardly offers" and no reasonable concessions. Steel strikes have been profitable for the union, which seems to be able to resist any public pressure to be reasonable, probably because the ordinary man is hit only indirectly by higher steel prices and is inclined to support pressure against the companies to give in. Little wonder that they should do so: they need to stop their losses, and the increased costs can be passed on to their customers.

The Teamsters Union, A.F. of L., offers an example of a modest toll paid the national union—only forty cents per member per month. Of course, this forty cents multiplied 1,300,000 times provides a very substantial revenue of $520,000 per month. Most of the Teamster strikes are local affairs, short lasting and not expensive, so the Teamsters can use their national revenue for such things as building and equipping, mechanically and humanly, a marble office building

107

in Washington that scowls across the plaza at the Senate wing of the Capitol. Teamster locals have a revenue of about $4,000,000 per month. It is plain that a monopoly controlling the employment of 1,300,000 men, with a stranglehold on every important industry directly or indirectly, and with an annual tax-free income of about $50,000,000, is a very powerful dictator of industrial policies—and a very profitable organization for those who run it.

The financial strength of the United Mine Workers monopoly is very difficult to estimate, for it is uncertain how many of its claimed 600,000 members pay dues and in what amounts. Minimum dues of $4.00 are required for locals, but no maximum limit is set. To the central office goes $2.00, and to the regional office goes $1.00, apparently providing annual incomes of $14,400,000 and $7,200,000 respectively. In addition, the U.M.W. has an enormous welfare fund, maintained and disbursed out of a tax on every ton of coal produced. Here is a union which, despite occasional rebels, has exercised an arbitrary control for years over an entire industry and is supported by an income ample to maintain a well-paid hierarchy and to discipline any rebels or backsliders.

Leaving the coal fields, we might find interest in the revenues of the Mine, Mill, and Smelter Workers, who have been "independent" since they were ousted from the C.I.O. for being communistic. Locals determine their dues within the limits of a minimum of $1.00 and a maximum of $5.00 per month and pay $1.00 per member per month to the national, giving it (according to a claimed membership of 100,000) an annual income of $1,200,000. How much of the local or national income is spent on strikes cannot be estimated; but the cost of one fairly long strike to the workers has been accurately estimated. This was the strike against Phelps Dodge at Bisbee, Douglas, and Morenci, Arizona. About 4,765 employees were idled for 30 working days, losing $83,435 each day in wages—or, for the 30-day strike, $2,503,050. Settlement of the strike brought an average increase in wages of fifteen cents an hour; but since the employees were offered an average increase of 12½ cents an hour before the strike, the actual strike gain was 2½ cents an hour. Dividing the total lost wages ($2,503,-050) by the daily increase for all 4,765 employees ($935.00), it appears that the employees must work 2,626 days to make up their lost wages out of their actual gain. If we figure six working days a week, they must work more than eight years!

This was only a small strike of a few thousand employees against one company; but it gives an indication of the colossal losses to the workers (to say nothing of losses to employers and the public) which are occasioned by a really big strike. Initially, such a strike may be financed by wealthy unions and borne by wealthy corporations. The enormous public and private losses which such a strike entails are the penalty which we have to pay for tolerating labor monopolies.

The use of dues by individual unions could be discussed for many pages, but to do so would only multiply examples of how far union coercive activities can be financed from only one of the three or four sources of union revenue. It seems needless to devote much time to initiation fees, although they produce a very handsome income to all unions. The amount of these fees is usually small in large unions, although they are large in some small unions. For instance, the initiation fee of the Steel Workers, C.I.O., is $5.00, while that of the Marine Engineers, C.I.O., is $250.00. Many of the large A.F. of L. unions have a fee of $5.00, but the Masters, Mates, and Pilots, A.F. of L. charges $200.00.

Far more important to maintenance of monopoly power than the funds collected from initiation fees is their use as a barrier to deny admission to a union on any terms. Such a use of initiation fees, along with stiff apprenticeship requirements, preserves many unions from any danger of competition by too many willing workers. The initiation fee is a very convenient weapon with which to maintain a monopoly of jobs, especially when its amount is determined by local unions unrestrained by constitutional limitations or regulations by the grand lodge; but it can be assumed that initiation fees count for much less in the overall power of union revenues than dues—or assessments.

Assessments are a method of raising money which is most effective and productive in a strongly disciplined union—especially in which compulsory unionism makes it impossible for a potential rebel to refuse to pay without losing his job. One major reason for an assessment is to prepare for a strike or to carry on a strike. Under these circumstances, obviously heavy pressure can be brought against unionists to accept an additional burden imposed by either national or local authority. Formerly assessments were often levied on members for political campaigns, either for friends or against enemies. Recently, because of laws forbidding direct political donations by unions (laws which are frequently evaded), there has developed a new form of assessment called a "contribution." To finance political campaigns, "educational" or "political action" organizations are created by national unions, and "contributions" are sought from all loyal unionists. It would be harder to raise money in this way were it not for the potent argument that this is just a way to evade an oppressive law passed to hamstring labor's political strength! It is contended that it is just as much the duty of a good union man to "contribute" as it is to pay dues or a regular assessment. It is also made clear to reluctant "contributors" that, if necessary, the same purposes can be accomplished by increasing dues or levying assessments to carry on such activities as issuing publications and sending officers to campaign. Politicians in public offices are likely to take a very broad view of what is not "political," especially when the activities in question benefit themselves or their friends.

From the preceding review of union revenues out of dues, initiation fees, assessments, and "contributions," it should be evident that organized labor in the United States does not suffer from lack of funds to carry on its monopolistic endeavors. Indeed, there is a grim humor in the complaints of labor unions against business lobbying in Washington. The labor unions themselves are by all odds the most powerful organizations that spend the most money trying to persuade or to bulldoze congressmen to vote for their private interests.

There is likewise grim humor in the constant complaint of the unions against alleged business monopolies, when the only widespread, long-standing, and effective monopolies in the business world are those maintained and constantly expanded by labor unions. Their legal exemption from prosecution, combined with a legal expenditure of vast sums of money and an illegal use of physical violence and terrorism, creates for them a monopolistic power which no business combination could possibly exercise.

11

Compulsory Unionism:
The New Slavery

For a generation all labor unions denounced "yellow dog contracts" under which employees were forced either to join a union approved by their employer or not to join any union. To free labor from such coercion these "yellow dog contracts" were made unlawful by national and state laws.

But today union labor leaders are demanding that a new variety of "yellow dog contract" be legalized. This is called a union shop agreement. Under such an agreement the employer forces every old and new employee to be a member, pay dues, and submit to the discipline of one particular union, or else lose his job. The union may be a good or bad union. It may

---

* This chapter is a slight expansion of an article in *Human Events* of July 2, 1955.

be loyal to the workers and to the government; or it may be a communist-controlled union disloyal to both.

The old laws prohibiting "yellow dog contracts" have been modified (at union demand) by national laws which permit an employer to make such a contract compelling membership in a union representing the majority of his employees of one craft or class. The only legal obstacles to the establishment of compulsory unionism and a monopoly of employments throughout the United States are: 1. The laws of seventeen states, which make it illegal either to compel a man to join a union in order to earn a living, or to prevent him from joining a union. 2. A provision in the Taft–Hartley Act which permits these state laws to be enforced, although, where there are no state laws, union closed shop contracts may be lawful. 3. The Constitution of the United States—under which the right of a man to earn a living without being compelled to pay tribute to a private organization, and the right of a man to join or refuse to join a private organization are guaranteed—and which *should* be and, let us hope, will be protected against private or public denial.

It is hard to understand how labor unions, which have developed, as voluntary organizations of self-help, to free labor from any oppressions of employer power, can justify their present program of using the employer's control of jobs to force men into unions to which they do not wish to belong.

The major arguments in behalf of compulsory unionism are as follows: 1. "Union security," that is, the strength of the *union,* depends upon universal acceptance of membership as a condition of employment. 2. Majority rule is a democratic principle, and a minority of workers who will not voluntarily support the union should be compelled to do so to solidify the power of the majority. 3. The union negotiates contracts for the benefit of all employees of a craft or class, and those who do not voluntarily contribute support to an organization which benefits them should be compelled to contribute. 4. The power of discipline over all workers should be available to the union so that it may insure the fulfillment of contracts and other assumed obligations.

Not one of the foregoing arguments can be maintained against the facts, nor can they justify the oppression and denial of individual liberty which is the inherent wrong of compulsory unionism.

1. It is a simple historical fact that the unions have increased in numbers and in economic and political power in the last twenty years as voluntary organiza-

tions, and under favoring national and state laws, they have no need to compel unwilling workers to join and pay them dues.

It is also hardly debatable that a voluntary organization of workers united for self-help is inherently a much stronger organization than a union composed to a considerable extent of unwilling members. Many of the strongest friends of organized labor have pointed out on many occasions that the strength of unionism in voluntary organizations would be greatly weakened by converting them into compulsory, monopolistic organizations which, if legally permitted, will inevitably require detailed regulation by government which would otherwise be unnecessary.

Two members of the National Defense Mediation Board, Judge Charles E. Wyzanski (former Solicitor of the Department of Labor) and former Senator Frank P. Graham, both made this point in opposition to compulsory unionism. President Franklin D. Roosevelt made a similar public pronouncement. Mr. Justice Frankfurter in the state "right-to-work" cases (335 U.S. 538) quoted extensively from the late Justice Brandeis, who held that "the ideal condition for a union is to be strong and stable, and yet to have in the trade outside its own ranks an appreciable number of men who are non-unionists. . . . Such a nucleus

117

of unorganized labor will check oppression by the unions as the unions check oppression by the employer."

2. "Majority democratic rule requires the minority to support the majority." This is a wholly fictitious argument because our laws and customs already require the minority of employees who are not members of a labor union to accept the terms and work under the contracts of the majority. This is similar to the requirement that any minority or dissenting group in a community must accept the laws enacted by the majority representatives. But, even in the case of public laws, a dissenting minority, a political party in opposition, is not required to stop its opposition; nor is it required to contribute to the political support of the majority party. Even members of the majority are at liberty to withdraw from such an association.

Those who espouse compulsory unionism are essentially adopting the communist theory that there should be only one party to which everyone should give allegiance and support. Inside the party there may be disagreements, but no one is permitted to go outside and support an opposition movement.

The claim of democratic majority rule by compulsory unionism is a pure fraud. Our democratic

118

theory of majority rule is based on the preservation of minority rights and minority opposition and the possibility of shifting the majority power. But when the workers are required to join and support a union regardless of their desire to oppose it, the whole democratic basis of majority rule disappears. It is supplanted by a monopoly rule which has no place in a democratic society and which, as a matter of fact, is a product of state socialism and communism.

3. The free rider argument: Much public stress is laid on the argument that, since the union negotiates for the benefit of all workers of a class, all such workers should be compelled to contribute to the cost of maintaining the union activities. This argument has a superficial appeal, but it is both fundamentally unsound and highly deceptive as to the facts.

The argument is *fundamentally unsound* because all through our society voluntary organizations carry on activities which benefit a great many who do not contribute any financial or other support. Fraternal organizations, churches, and civic and political organizations raise money, organize work, and carry it on for the benefit of a large number of persons who contribute no support. How absurd it would be to suggest that whenever a voluntary organization benefits any

119

group of people it should be empowered to compel them by law or by economic pressure to contribute support!

The argument is also *highly deceptive* for three reasons. First, only a part of the dues and assessments of the unions is devoted to negotiating contracts. The unions have a great many activities such as political campaigns, social and economic propaganda, insurance, and so forth, to which no one should be compelled to contribute, particularly when he himself is not convinced that they are for his benefit. Second, the real objective of forcing all workers to join unions is, as the union leaders themselves admit, not so much to compel them to pay their share of an expense, as to compel them to accept the discipline of the organization and, by concerted actions and the appearance of increased numbers, add to the economic and political power of the union. Third, the unions sought and obtained by law a *special privilege*—the right to represent any minority of non-member employees and to make contracts binding on any such minority. The unions took away by law the right and freedom of individual employees to contract for themselves—and now the unions demand that non-members be compelled to pay for having their freedom of contract taken away and exercised against their will! The non-

120

member is not a "free rider"; he is a captive passenger.

4. The need of an increased power of discipline: This argument, which is being made with increasing vehemence, is based on the theory that non-union employees, who cannot be disciplined by depriving them of their employment, are a menace both to the union and to the employer because they will not live up to contract obligations. Here again is a fraudulent argument because the non-union employees is just as much bound as the union employee to carry out the obligations of the trade agreement.

Also, without being made a member of the union the independent worker is subject to employer discipline to an even greater degree than a union member. If he breaks contract obligations, or refuses to obey management orders, he can be and will be disciplined by the employer, and he will not have any union backing to support him in a recalcitrant position. On the other hand, if a union man gets in difficulty with the management, the union is obligated to support him if it can. What the unions really mean is that they want the power of discipline over all employees, particularly so that they will all strike, or otherwise support the union officials in whatever position they may take which is antagonistic to management. The fact is that the increased power of discipline given to union officials by compulsory unionism is all contrary to the interest of both the employer and the free worker.

There are various other arguments brought forward by the unions in the effort to prove that a worker is better off as a compulsory member than if he is allowed to remain voluntarily a non-member. For instance, the A.F. of L. contends that if the employee is not a union man "he has no voice at all in determining his rate of pay, his hours or other conditions of employment." Theoretically, this appears to be plausible. But as a practical fact the union member of one of the huge unions of modern times has as small a voice in determining union policies and programs as the average citizen who is not active in politics has in making the laws. The most effective voice which any man can have in an organization, unless he is a part of the ruling hierarchy, is the voice of opposition, the voice of criticism. This may be a small voice, but one which can be made effective only if it is coupled with the power to withdraw from the organization, to refuse to give it moral and financial support, and to threaten unwise or vicious leadership with the development of a rival faction or organization to challenge its authority.

The major value of labor organizations to the workers lies in their power to control their representatives. They may become helpless subjects of a labor autocracy if the individual worker is denied the right and freedom to refuse to support an official or an organization which does not truly represent him. How much should a man rely on the servant he employs, who then assumes to be his master and says, "You must obey me or I will cut your throat?"

Let us review briefly a few other union arguments against "right-to-work" laws. The unions claim these laws are an "anti-labor weapon." How can a law be "anti-labor" which provides only that an employee shall be absolutely free from employer coercion either to join or not to join a union? How can a law sustaining the freedom of labor be honestly called an "anti-labor" law? The unions are actually claiming that it is against the interests of the worker to be free from employer coercion! They are claiming that if the union approves of employer coercion, then it is "anti-labor" to insist that the employee be kept free from any tyrannical use of the employer's power, against which union labor claims to be the ancient, time-honored enemy!

The agreement for a union closed shop is now called a "union security" agreement. This very designation is a confession that it is not the *worker* who is made more *secure* by union closed shop agreements. In fact, he is made utterly dependent upon a tyrannical control of his livelihood, exercised jointly by the employer and the union. Only the union itself—that is, the union officialdom—is made more "secure" by such agreements. These closed shop contracts, these "one party" monopolies, make it practically impossible for dissenters, even for a substantial majority, in the union successfully to oppose the dictatorial control of a well-entrenched machine of labor bosses.

In practical result, the union closed shop agreement destroys the fundamental principle of self-organization and collective bargaining which, during the twentieth century, friends and organizers of free labor have been establishing firmly in public opinion, public policy, and public law.

The Railway Labor Act (1926, 1934), the Wagner Act (1935), and the Taft–Hartley Act (1947) in the same language established in all industries subject to federal law the right of all employees to "self-organization" and "to bargain collectively through representatives of their own choosing"—and the right to exercise these rights free from employer "interference, influence or coercion." How can there possibly be "self-organization" or "representatives of their own choosing" when men and women are compelled to join unions against their will? How can there be freedom from employer "interference, influence or coercion" when every employee is forced by his employer to join the particular union with which the employer has made a union shop agreement?

The union bosses argue that every employee is free to select *within the union* his representative. But this is not a genuine freedom of choice, any more than there is freedom of voting under a communist government. In communism there is only "one party" which the voter can choose to represent him. In compulsory unionism there is only "one party" which the employee can choose to represent him. The single, helpless voter under compulsory communism has no free choice of his legal representative.

There can be no self-organization or self-government, no government by consent of the governed, when persons are not free either to join or to refuse to join or to withdraw from the organization or the party which has the legal authority to represent them, to speak for them, and to make agreements binding on them. In the language of Chief Justice Hughes, upholding the constitutionality of the Railway Labor

Act (281 U.S. 548), "Collective action would be a mockery if representation were made futile by interference with freedom of choice."

The outstanding labor unions of the United States are making a mockery out of collective bargaining and destroying the essential freedom of labor by their campaign to establish compulsory unionism which should not be lawful under a free government or tolerated by a free people.

12

Industry-Wide Bargaining

FROM TIME to time a question is raised as to whether industry-wide bargaining should not be forbidden. Contracts between the employers representing practically or actually an entire industry and a single union representing at least a majority of all the employees are clearly monopolistic in character and in consequences. But the answer is not a simple one.

There are many advantages in such contracts to all concerned. Employers avoid a competitive struggle to establish economical wages and working conditions. Employees gain better wages and conditions on the average than they could probably gain in a competitive struggle. There may be some advantages to the public and consumers, but these are certainly overweighed by their inevitable exploitation by any monopolistic control of industry.

There are definite disadvantages to the employers in the loss of opportunities for high-cost producers to keep down labor costs, and of the opportunities for low-cost producers to obtain the most efficient labor by offering better wages and conditions than competitors. The more efficient workers as individuals certainly have the disadvantage of not being able to command higher pay and better conditions when all contracts are standardized.

There can be no doubt that the consuming public suffers from industry-wide bargaining, because competition in labor costs goes far to insure full value received for the consumer's dollar.

Reference has been made heretofore to the monopolistic contract forced by the electrical workers and employers in the New York City area. It may be assumed that the employers supplying electrical goods were not entirely unwilling to have a local monopoly established for them; but there is no question as to the increased prices which consumers were thus forced to pay. If such monopolistic contracts are expanded through industry-wide bargaining to cover all metropolitan areas, or the entire nation, the result must be, as the Supreme Court expressed it, "to shift our society from a competitive to a monopolistic economy."

However, we cannot assume that a steady and pro-
128

nounced shift of this character will continue many years without a demand for some such congressional action as the Court envisaged as the only available remedy. If the monopolistic powers of labor unions are steadily extended, it seems inevitable that this demand will eventually subject all industry-wide bargaining and contracts to supervision and regulation, just as public service monopolies are supervised and regulated by state and federal commissions.

Even now there would be a manifest absurdity in unregulated public-utility labor relations if, for example, all electric utilities and one big union of electrical workers made uniform contracts which all the regulatory bodies had to accept as one of the bases for rates. Fortunately collective bargaining is still localized in this industry, and separate employers negotiate with separate, largely autonomous, unions. It is significant that in the one case of a regulated industrial monopoly where there is often nation-wide, or at least regional, bargaining, the unions (which have generally local autonomy) are all subject to a national supervisory and mildly regulatory law, the Railway Labor Act.

The many objections voiced by other unions to the mild limitations on union freedom of action imposed by the Railway Labor Act show how deeply organized labor would resent any attempt to regulate their activities sufficiently to avoid the abuse of their monopolistic powers. But, if regulation is not acceptable and unregulated monopoly becomes intolerable, how should the legislative power of the government be exerted to restore and preserve that competition which the unions are so determined to destroy?

It would be no answer to this question to require by law that all negotiations and contracts be limited to one employer and his employees. In the first place, such a limitation would undermine the whole theory of unionization which finds it necessary to have a labor organization extend beyond the domain of a single employer to unite all workers of a common interest in a community of activity. In the second place, the mere form of separate negotiations would not prevent the pressure for, and adoption of, standardized contracts. It makes little difference whether the steel workers negotiate with a dozen companies at once or with a dozen separately. The union representatives are going to stick together for one contract just as long as they are legally free to do so.

The simple fact is that there is no good way to legislate effectively against the *unhealthy* exercise of monopoly powers so long as any exercise of monopoly powers is permitted. It would undoubtedly be very desirable to permit business managements to get together and agree on "codes of fair competition," to eliminate unfair and shady practices that do no one except sharpers any good. But, as the writer acutely remembers, this is precisely what N.R.A. tried to do, and it has been denounced for over twenty years as "fascist" and "legalized monopoly."

Consequently, to get rid of the abuse of monopoly powers by business managers, we have found it necessary to insist on maintaining a law forbidding all contracts in restraint of trade, to attack all creations of monopoly power, even to the extent of preventing mergers and acquisitions which may threaten the creation of monopoly power. It seems evident that, to meet the growing similar menace of labor union monopolies, we should seriously face the need of preventing their creation. We should challenge the union creed that monopoly is an essential objective of any labor organization with a new doctrine that monopoly shall not be a legal objective of any labor organization.

What this new doctrine really means is a curtailment of the power of the central organization of a national or international union. We may start with the concept that the essential right of employees is to organize for collective bargaining with their employer. Then we will find that these local organizations need to be federated in industry-wide or national organizations to gain strength and independence from the excessive bargaining power of the employer. The next logical step would be the development of a federation of autonomous locals, but instead there has arisen the concept of a national union which creates local unions as agencies to carry out its purposes. This illogical concept of the function of a national union, which makes inevitable an attempt to establish monopoly, must be destroyed.

One way of doing so would be by the enactment of an anti-union-monopoly law. Such a law would recognize that the essential freedom of labor requires acceptance of the right of all employees of any employer to organize for concerted action, and that these unions should be free to cooperate and affiliate with other unions of common interest to achieve legitimate objectives. But it would permit no combination of unions, either by federation or by uniting in a national union, to exercise such control over a local union as to take away its freedom and its obligation to bargain and contract solely with a single employer and only in behalf of its employees. The law would provide that any contract, procedure, or practice in restraint of the autonomy of a union to bargain or contract in behalf of the employees of a single employer should be held monopolistic and unlawful. It would further provide that any combination of unions, or creation of a union representing employees of more than one employer, which was found guilty of unlawful restraint of local union autonomy, should be required by judicial decree to cease and desist, or in case of failure to comply with such a decree, should be dissolved.

It has not been the purpose of this writing to propose any such sweeping attack on the monopolistic evils of industry-wide bargaining, but merely to point out how drastic an alteration of present concepts would be necessary to deal with this problem effectively. It is possible that milder legislative deterrents of monopoly power, if attempted, may well put a healthy stop to present unhealthy trends. But before suggesting a few moderate remedies it is necessary to examine more closely the increasing political activities of all the major labor organizations.

13

The Prospect of a Labor Government

THE STEADY drive of the unions to dominate
one or both political parties is a phenomenon of comparatively recent years. Labor's increasing political
power makes its increasing monopolistic economic
power doubly dangerous. In this unhealthy combination of powers for the benefit of one large segment of
the population, we have in fact a drive toward a "dictatorship of the proletariat" portending a socialistic
control of both government and industry, which must
be in the end destructive of the foundations of the
free enterprise system and the prosperity of the American people.

The purpose of the outstanding leaders of organized labor to establish a socialist labor government of
the United States is becoming more evident every
day. Listen to this argument made by the American

Federation of Labor in a case which the writer argued against before the Supreme Court of the United States: "The worker becomes a member of an economic society when he takes employment. . . . The union is the organization or government of this society. . . . It has in a sense the powers and responsibilities of a government."

You do not need to be a communist to know that in order to govern such an economic society you must control the political government of this society. This is well understood by our modern labor leaders, and their immediate program to increase their political power has two principal objectives: first, to unite all labor organizations either in one federation or at least in a concert of action to have laws enacted which favor union labor; and second, to repeal all the state laws that forbid a union closed shop and then force all employers everywhere to agree not to hire or to retain any employee who does not join a union, pay its dues, and submit to its discipline.

There is nothing imaginary or uncertain about this determination of union officials to acquire and maintain a monopoly power over all industrial employments. To quote again from the Supreme Court argument of the A.F. of L.: "We can summarize the nature of union membership as a common condition of employment in an industrial society by again comparing it to citizenship in a political society. Both are compulsory upon individuals."

Some people may think that compulsion to join a private union as a universal requirement before any willing worker is allowed to earn a living would be a violation of fundamental freedoms which are constitutionally guaranteed to all Americans; but union labor has a short answer to that contention. To quote again from the A.F. of L. argument: "The liberty of the individual is not the right to license, but participation in a social organization founded upon equality, justice and law. The union is that organization for employees."

To put this in simple language, it appears, according to this labor argument, that the liberty of an American worker does not include a right to refuse to join a union, but only the right to be a member of a union. However, even this peculiar liberty does not include a right to join any union the worker chooses because, under a union shop agreement, he must join the particular union which made the agreement with his employer, or else lose his job.

It may also be noted that all kinds of unions are included in the description of a "social organization founded upon equality, justice and law." Perhaps one may wonder whether various communist-ruled unions merit such a flattering description. One may wonder whether unions which have been run by notorious extortioners and other unions ruled by violent and tyrannical bosses should be classified as exemplars of "equality, justice and law."

It is strange, however, that whenever trade unions are under discussion in legislatures, executive offices, or in the courts, all liberals are expected to assume that all unions are essentially noble in purpose, angelic in operation, and admirable in their objectives. If anyone criticizes the vicious practices that disgrace all too many unions he is denounced as an enemy of labor. Now, as a matter of plain fact, unions even at their best, are simply organizations of men and women who by concerted action are trying to make a better living for themselves under better conditions. This is also the aim of many other organizations that make no claim to holy virtue and immunity from criticism.

But there is a vast difference between those voluntary organizations whose members can resign if they don't like their policies or their management, and a closed shop union whose members are compelled to support union policies and union bosses, or lose their livelihood.

137

The most fundamentally wrong attitude of labor leaders today is their plain intention to establish a compulsory membership and an unlimited governing power in what should be a voluntary society. The development of societies of human beings to work together for common benefit is what has raised man from animalism to civilization. Even a voluntary society must have some sort of internal government. But any government is the power of a ruling class to lay down laws and force others to obey them, and more government than is absolutely necessary is an evil that changes the happiness and efficiency of willing cooperation into an unhappy submission to an oppressive servitude.

Of course as long as membership in a society is voluntary, some restraints of individual liberty are not oppressive and are necessary to prevent the disorder and destructive results of anarchistic freedom. In a voluntary society of scientists or businessmen or workers a great deal of discipline will be gladly accepted. But if the private government of such a society forces needless or unfair obligations and restrictions on the members they can always regain individual freedom by resigning.

Unfortunately, the creation of any society such as a community, a nation, or a union develops a governing

138

class that inevitably seeks to increase its power. Sometimes this desire for power rises from apparently laudable motives, ambitions to make people happier, more prosperous, or more virtuous. These intentions are always claimed by rising rulers. Sometimes power hunger is just a base desire for power itself, an ambition to rule the lives of others for personal profit or glory. These intentions are never admitted. The corrupting influence of power is one of the few positive laws that every social scientist should recognize.

For centuries human beings, for mutual aid and protection, formed economic and political societies of every conceivable character. Merchants and traders, workers and fighters, communities and nations were organized. As these societies grew larger their governments became bigger and more powerful—and more tyrannical. Then the demand for individual freedom, which seems to be born in every human being, became strong enough to challenge all the old concepts of a compulsory society governed by a divinely qualified ruling class. A free society of free men maintained by a free government became the objective of millions of people.

Here in America it seemed for many decades that such a society with a free government of limited powers was being achieved. The only challenges to our ideal of individual liberty, the only demand for un-limited government, came from a small number of socialists whose program to make everyone dependent on an all-powerful state had little appeal to the pros-pering millions of free Americans. Then we were forced by a great depression and two world wars into tremendous expansions of government power which we had always opposed. Voices of protest were de-nounced as voices of reaction. We were told that more and more government, more and more forceful disci-pline, less and less individual liberty, were inevitable. Whether we listened to fascists, communists, or those milder socialists who called themselves "liberals," we were told that all-powerful governments were coming irresistibly on the wave of the future.

In the last twenty years of this period the political power of organized labor has grown steadily with its vast increase of economic power. Ambitious labor union officials, both the best and the worst, have de-veloped Napoleonic concepts of making the political power of big government subservient to big labor. They seek to control government immediately as their ally, and eventually as their servant. The older union policy of voting for friends and against enemies, but avoiding political partisanship, has been abandoned. The modern policy is to put heavy pressures to support labor programs on all parties and candidates and then to deliver all possible votes to the party and candidates bidding the highest for union favor.

The political machines of organized labor have not been developing a labor party, which would be a minority party, but have been working shrewdly toward a labor-dominated party which would have majority power. The labor partisanship of all the national administrations from 1935 to 1953 increased enormously both the size and the influence of labor unions. Labor politicians found in the veiled socialism of the growing welfare state a political program which appealed to millions of voters like farmers, small businessmen, and white-collar workers, who would not previously follow labor leadership.

The strategy of increasing union labor's political power was obvious. The Democratic party could not be completely converted into a socialist labor party, because in some areas its historical devotion to local self-government and its distrust of centralized power still survived—particularly in the South. The Republican party could not be completely condemned and abandoned because it had segments and leaders whose conversion to welfare state socialism would help to counterbalance the unconverted sections of the Democratic party.

So the strategy for achieving a socialist labor government still required bi-partisan activities. The majority support of Democratic socializers must be maintained and a minority support from Republican socializers obtained wherever possible. Future prospects and the present political situation emphasize the wisdom of this bipartisan development of labor's political power.

At present writing we have a Republican President who, despite his earlier vigorous opposition to a welfare state, has advanced many welfare state projects—as, for example, social insurance, federal control of education, and federal public works—to an extent worthy of more union labor applause than has been given. Of course in many ways the Eisenhower administration is far from satisfactory to a socialist labor leadership. It is too friendly to free enterprise. The President does not espouse all union programs, and may well oppose some of them. When his Secretary of Labor openly advocated compulsory unionism, the President said that the Secretary spoke for himself alone.

We have a Democratic Congress. But, there are many Republicans in Congress who are easily persuaded by union labor arguments and many Democrats who are not always subservient to union demands. So it is still a sound strategy to make sure in a bi-partisan government that union labor can always command a bi-partisan majority in its favor on crucial issues. Of course more pro-labor legislation and pro-labor law enforcement is always desired, but the prevention of any government action to free industry from organized labor violence, coercion, and monopoly is most important to maintain the economic power of the labor unions, and this they have accomplished during many years through bi-partisan political support.

So long as we allow labor unions to use brutal force, to paralyze vital industries, and to compel great business enterprises to yield to demands that are unfair and injurious to the public, the union bureaucrats will be able to maintain their private tyrannies superior to any effective restraint by our public government. These are indeed the only private organizations that are permitted to carry out vicious conspiracies against public and private interests in open disregard of the laws that elsewhere protect the lives, business, and property of a free people.

It is not surprising that such a favored class now seeks openly to establish a compulsory society under their personal government to which all workers must submit. Already the unionists have been authorized

143

by federal laws to fortify their private autocracies with union shop contracts under which every worker must pay them tribute and become subject to their rule.

It should be evident from the union campaign against state right-to-work laws that union officials are not sure they can continue to persuade more and more workers to join their huge unions. These unions are so large that the average member is far more helpless to protect himself against union tyranny than he was years ago helpless to protect himself against a hard employer. In olden days he had a chance to get another job. How can he get a job today when blacklisted by a monopolizing union?

Most union men today understand how helpless they are as individuals to control union policy, or even to have their ideas or complaints fairly considered. They have one of two choices. They can just remain voiceless and accept the inevitable, as many citizens accept bad city government. Or they can resign from the union if this will not deprive them of every opportunity to earn a living. Of course if and when there is a union monopoly of the employments for which they are fitted they will probably submit to compulsory unionism rather than starve.

Nevertheless, there is plenty of evidence that high union officials are worried by two things. One is any

144

competition between unions. The other is any competition between union workers and independent
workers. They want to end both competitions. First,
they would stop the unions from competing for members. Second, they would end the competition between workers by making all workers submissive
members of non-competing unions. The A.F. of L.
argument in the Supreme Court, to which I have
previously referred, made this desire and policy plain
in the extraordinary contention that—"workers cannot thrive but can only die under competition between themselves."

It is a curious fact that for thousands of years workers have been competing with one another without
dying, but with better living as a consequence. Despite labor organizations that from time to time have
sought to limit or end competition between workers
they have, under persistent competition, steadily improved their abilities and increased their productiv-
ity. With the aid of machines and other managerial
devices to increase productive capacity, which labor
organizations have usually opposed, the persistent
competition of workers with workers has brought
about an average standard of living incomparably
higher than was even imagined in ancient days. The
greatest restraint on the continuing increase of the

workers' productive capacity is imposed today by uniform union wages and rules which are designed to end this beneficient competition. Yet, in disregard of economic history, outstanding labor leaders try to make us believe that "workers can only die under competition."

The real fear of labor officials appears to be that the power and profit of their offices may be diminished or even die under competition for voluntary support. They fear to have the value of their services tested by competition. Their customary claim is that practically all union members are loyal supporters of their union bosses and that only the non-union man is a menace to union solidarity. But now and then an authoritative unionist reveals the truth, which is that the object of compulsory unionism is not only to bring in new members but to establish a power of discipline over old members as well. This was the frank admission made to a Senate committee and then to a Presidential emergency board by George M. Harrison, President of the Railway Clerks, and a notable labor politician.

We may sympathize with the difficulties of the officials of any voluntary organization—difficulties in getting agreement upon policies and programs and

146

then in advancing them by orderly concerted action. But do we think that these difficulties should be relieved by making membership in a church or a civic association or a fraternal organization compulsory? Or do we believe that among a free people only voluntary societies, only unions which are privately governed by the consent of the governed, should be tolerated, and that compulsory unionism should be as unlawful as other forms of involuntary servitude?

Many people, including even some large employers, do not appreciate the vast difference between the present campaign for a universal compulsory unionism and the negotiation in by-gone years of many closed shop contracts. In the days when competition between many employers and between many unions left many doors of employment open to independent workers, there was no labor monopoly established by such contracts. There was no threat of the concentration of dangerous economic and political power in the hands of a union autocracy. Frequently an employer was only seeking industrial peace by ending union rivalries when he signed an exclusive contract with one union. The repeated claim of the unions today is that labor monopolies will bring peace. The establishment of a business monopoly will likewise end com-

147

petitive strife. But a labor monopoly as well as a business monopoly can bring only the peace of submission to dictatorial power.

Today the union bureaucracies are plainly seeking supreme economic and political power. The union closed shop contract is a weapon of awesome force in that battle for power. The prospect of a socialist labor government is not remote. It would be clearly an early prospect except for two retarding factors. One is the rivalries and jealousies that still divide union labor and hamper the concentrated exertion of its united strength. The other retarding factor is the disillusion spreading among the American people, first, as to the unselfish virtue of labor unions and labor leaders, and, second, disillusion as to the comfort and security of life in the socialized welfare state which organized labor is promoting.

One may hope that it is not too late to convince a majority of the American people that they do not want, and that their children will hate, the socialistic laws which are being forced upon us in wider circles and greater depth every year. But our great difficulty in making this demonstration is that the fear of foreign aggression and tyranny is being used again as the basis for calming other fears and stifling all objections to the aggressive imposition of more and more domestic tyranny, and the loss of more and more personal liberty.

This does not mean that we should underestimate the threat or the evil of communism. It only means that the possibility of a physical conquest of the United States by communist force is not so immedaite a danger as the mental conquest of the United States by socialist persuasion. State socialism is the fundamental creed of communism. We will never save the soul of America, we will never preserve the freedom of the American people, by sacrificing our lives and our treasure to prevent the forceful imposition of international socialism if we are persuaded to accept peacefully the same sort of government, imposed on us by United Nations treaties and by federal laws expanding our national welfare state.

The well-advertised Marxian way to create an all-powerful socialist state is to use labor organizations as the means of gaining an economic dictatorship out of which the political "dictatorship of the proletariat" can then be achieved. The recent rapid progress of such a program in the United States should warn us that the prospect of a socialist labor government (under a less offensive label) is a very real and threatening menace to the maintenance of our constitutional form of government and our constitutional liberties.

14

Some Remedies for Labor Monopoly Evils

A NOTABLE musician once described a fugue as a piece of music in which the theme keeps coming in and the audience keeps going out. Discussing labor relations is like a fugue. Strikes keep coming in and the workers keep going out.

But the strikes of fifty years ago were vastly different from the strikes of today. Those old-fashioned strikes were usually local—brawls between a small group of employees and their employer. They might be viciously and unfairly fought, but they were man-to-man fights for a definite personal victory. They were part of the competitive struggle between individuals. Despite socialist oratory they were not outbreaks of class warfare. The overwhelming majority of wage earners believed in a competitive economy.

The insidious poison of what is called democratic socialism had not infected masses of our people.

The important strikes of today are utterly different in purpose, in methods, and in results. Let us not deceive ourselves. They are part of a class warfare that has been spreading like a prairie fire across the whole world. We deny that there is any class warfare in the United States; but we prove it by writing hundreds of laws and thousands of rules for waging economic wars, while we fumble over futile programs for settling these conflicts peacefully.

A strike that shuts down the water transportation of a city like New York or stops all milk deliveries in a metropolitan area is not even a strike against employers as a class. Nor is a strike against steel, or coal, or transportation merely a strike against employers. These are warfare by a class against the community. Such strikes make no sense except as moves in a revolution to establish class domination. Sober economists question whether labor has made any gains in excess of its losses by such strikes; whether at least it has made any gains which could not have been obtained without strikes.

But no program to outlaw all strikes would be practical, if one were wise. It would be folly to advocate any program of forbidding or preventing all strikes. If it were possible politically to do this, the result would be to force labor into more violent efforts to preserve its ultimate weapon against tyrannies of property power. The time has come, however, when we should recognize that, just as property power, grown excessive, had to be offset by labor and political power, so organized labor power, grown excessive, must now be offset by public power and private property power.

In a recent notable address the late Justice Jackson pointed out that: "It is the nature of power always to resist and evade restraints by law, just as it is the essential nature of law, as we know it, always to curb power." He went on to state that: "The conception of law as a brake on power is one of the chief contributions to civilization made by our [the legal] profession."

In this address, delivered at the laying of the cornerstone of the American Bar Center, Justice Jackson made an extraordinary summary of the creed of the legal profession from which only the following sentences are quoted as particularly pertinent to the present discussion:

"We believe in law as an intellectual discipline capable of directing the thought and action of law-trained men and, through their leadership, of guiding men and masses away from violence, vengeance and force and toward submission of all grievances to settlement by fair legal procedures. . . .

"We believe that the only permissible use of coercive force is under the law. No device of compulsion by public authority or private advantage is tolerable unless authorized by the law of the land and executed by procedures that conform to strict concepts of due processes of law."

We are facing now the need of applying a rule of law in the domain of what have been called economic conflicts between management and labor. This necessity has come about because of the inevitable trend of the presently increased power of organized labor toward what must be in the end a class rule, which must be in the end a dictatorial rule.

Under our democratic-republican form of government with its preservation of individual liberty, the standard of living and the general welfare in the United States have risen beyond even the dreams of previous generations. To preserve these we must put brakes upon the power of the rulers of organized labor to dominate the entire economy and politics of the nation. Those rulers of organized labor, if they were wise, would themselves approve of putting brakes upon powers which are rapidly getting beyond the capacity of any rulers to wield wisely, or even safely.

153

Wide publicity has been given to proposals which the writer made not long ago to restrict the powers of organized labor, particularly in the matter of striking.* So it seems worth while now to explain further what was offered as "a practical program of obvious remedies for intolerable abuses of labor's powers of collective action"—powers which "should be preserved but in particular uses must be restrained."

Proposition 1. "The creation and exercise of monopoly powers by labor unions should be made unlawful." The reason for the exemption of labor unions from the prohibitions and penalties of the antitrust laws was not because anyone contended that labor unions should be permitted to exercise monopoly powers. It was because in their normal efforts to establish uniform terms and conditions of employment unions might be and often were held to be technically "conspiracies in restraint of trade." Hence the provision was written into the law that in the legitimate exercise of their legitimate functions labor unions should not be held conspiracies in restraint of trade.

Unfortunately, aided by judicial constructions, this

---

* See *Reader's Digest,* January, 1954.

limited exemption of labor unions has been unduly extended into a wholesale exemption of all their activities from prosecution as monopolistic. As a result, the unions openly take the position that their now declared object to monopolize all employments has been legalized and that they have a right to exercise monopoly controls over jobs and wages, and over the quality, quantity, and price of products. This means that, the greater the power of the unions, the greater becomes their monopoly control of the entire economy, with the eventual destruction of a competitive economy becoming inevitable with the constant rise of labor power. There is no possibility of preserving a free economy unless the exercise of such monopoly powers by organized labor is clearly made unlawful.

Proposition 2. "Compulsory unionism, a form of involuntary servitude, should be abolished by law. This is a duty of Congress under the Thirteenth Amendment."

Fifty years ago, when the closed shop was only an agreement between a single employer and a group of employees, the requirement that every employee in one plant should be a member of a local union would not impose involuntary servitude on any one, because there were plenty of competing enterprises where a man could get a job without joining a union. The closed shop was then an exception and the open shop the rule.

Today, when unions have enlarged to huge numbers and the coverage of union contracts is often industry-wide, the requirement that a man must join a union in order to obtain a particular employment has become in fact a requirement that he must join a union, a private organization, in order to be able to work. In one industry after another the door has been closed to the employment of any except union members.

It is a simple fact today that compulsory unionism is a denial to millions of men of any ability to earn a living except by agreeing to pay dues and submit to the discipline of a private organization. They cannot even withdraw from a labor union if violently opposed to its economic or political policies without losing the ability to earn a livelihood. This is in reality an involuntary servitude which it is not only the right but the duty of the Congress under the Thirteenth Amendment to forbid by law.

Proposition 3. "The right to strike should be qualified and limited by defining the lawful objects, the lawful methods, and the lawful occasions for strikes. Strikes should be held unlawful which are:

156

"Strikes against the public health, safety, and welfare.

"Strikes to compel political action.

"Strikes without a preceding reasonable effort to avoid a strike.

"Strikes conducted with the aid or toleration of criminal violence."

It may be easy to make the foregoing statements, but the question immediately arises: Suppose a law is passed making such wrongful strikes unlawful? In the first place, how will the law be enforced? In the second place, how will the economic conflicts be settled which will still inevitably arise?

The answer to the first question is not a difficult one. Senator Taft once asked me, in a discussion about outlawing certain strikes, how you were going to put ten thousand men in jail? I answered him that that would never be necessary. A large effective strike requires organization and leadership. There are very few spontaneous mass uprisings. Generally, even rioting has organization behind it. To prevent lawless collective action, all that is necessary is to strike at the leadership and centers of organization of any such mass movement.

Certainly the communists have taught us this lesson, even if they have done it in a most vicious and

157

indefensible manner. But, the government anti-strike action against John L. Lewis and the United Mine Workers should have settled the question for all time that a vigorous government can, with due process of law, peacefully prevent, or at least make ineffective, any lawful strike.

The second question is a much more serious one. Certainly a strike against the public health, safety, and welfare should be subject to prevention. On the other hand, those who are engaged in rendering services, as in public utilities, which are essential to the public health, safety, and welfare, should not be left subject to the dictation of private management as to the terms and conditions of their employment. Their just grievances should have a full opportunity of just settlement.

Here, however, we find a curious inconsistency in public thinking. It has been long accepted that the rates and conditions of public service can be regulated by government tribunals. Why, therefore, should not the wages and conditions of employment be likewise regulated? The stock answer is that "property rights," such as payments for, and protection of capital can be submitted to judicial tribunals, but that "human rights" to wages and working conditions should not be subject to any such determination.

In the first place, it should be pointed out that fixing rates and service conditions in a public utility is not merely determining the rights of investors, but also the very important rights, the "human rights" if you will, of thousands of consumers who are absolutely dependent upon public utility services. They are certainly as vitally interested in proper utility rates as wage earners are in proper wages. Furthermore, the standards by which fair wages for labor can be determined are about as easily ascertained and can be as impartially applied as the standards fixing payments for capital and fair rates for utility service.

As a final answer, however, to all those who object to any judicial settlement of wages and working conditions in industries of public necessity, I may suggest that anyone who engages as his livelihood in an industry of vital necessity has taken for himself the security of an employment upon which his fellow citizens are definitely dependent. He should accept an obligation to give continuous service. Furthermore, even public utility services are competitive to some extent with other services. Prices should not be forced up indefinitely by increased labor costs. Consumers use more electricity because it is cheap. They use less coal and more oil for fuel partly because John L. Lewis and his followers have used monopoly power so unwisely as to price their product out of many markets. Milk is a necessity to some, but a luxury, as the price goes up, to others.

However, it is not my proposition that any law should require the compulsory arbitration of all labor disputes in essential industries. Representatives of management and labor should not only have opportunity, but be required to make every reasonable effort, to agree upon terms and conditions of employment. But if, because of disagreement and the absence of a contract under which cooperation can continue, the public is threatened with a stoppage in production or distribution of an essential commodity or service, then there should be a recognized public right to intervene and to insure for a brief period, such as six months or one year, a continuation of production either with or without modification of the existing contract.

Such a law would not impose any involuntary servitude because no worker would be required to continue his employment. But it should be a provision of the law that any worker quitting his work would be acting as an individual, resigning all present and future rights, as he would in any permanent quitting of employment. It would also be unlawful to conduct or maintain any concerted withdrawal of employment or boycott of the business involved. As a practical matter, we may be sure that the vast majority of American workers, unionized or non-unionized, would welcome and live happily under a law which lifted from them the burdens and losses of strikes. I venture the prophecy that those industries in which striking had been practically outlawed would become rapidly among the most preferred of employments.

Political strikes. There should be no argument among believers in the American form of government that strikes to compel political action should be outlawed. The idea of converting an economic organization into a political organization has grown recently, but has still not grown to the point where the American worker desires to find himself hazarding his livelihood from time to time and stopping his earning power in the effort to compel a political action regarding which he may be far from enthusiastic. Furthermore, the attempt to coerce public officials by concerted attacks on the public welfare is a subversive attack upon our form of government.

Quickie strikes. As a principle, most persons will agree that strikes without a preceding reasonable effort to avoid a strike are an intolerable wrong on all three parties concerned. First of all, on the worker; second, on the management; and third, on the consuming public. Nevertheless, in recent years there have been plagues of petty strikes throughout industries, which clearly show the need for putting a brake upon the abuse of power by little men vested with a brief authority. Penalizing such strikes should be a matter of easy legislation and prosecution.

Lawless violence. What to do about a strike conducted with the aid or toleration of criminal violence is a more complicated problem. It is entirely possible for *agents provocateurs* or outsiders to take advantage of a strike situation and to "frame" a law-abiding labor organization with charges of criminality. Nevertheless, it is not unreasonable to require that any organization conducting a strike take every reasonable means of preventing criminal violence. Nor is it difficult, as a rule, to distinguish a labor organization which lives by and with the aid of violence from one which is essentially law-abiding.

Under the cloak of unionism, so many vicious, intolerable criminal organizations have flourished that it should be made to the interest of all legitimate labor organizations to dissociate themselves from such criminality. Contrariwise, at the present time there is far too close association and cooperation between organizations of a fundamentally criminal character

162

and those which are primarily law-abiding, but entirely willing to be the beneficiaries of lawlessness.

Fifty years ago, when labor unions were struggling even to gain the right of recognition and struggling against vicious lawless tactics of many employers and employer organizations, there was much excuse if not justification for the use of hoodlums, sluggers, and even worse criminals by those who felt they were fighting for the underdog against overwhelming respectable but tyrannical power. Today, there is little excuse for criminality in support of the legitimate activities of labor unions. It would be far better for the health of labor and for its public relations if outstanding labor leaders supported instead of opposed laws intelligently designed to prevent racketeering and criminality under cloak of labor organizations.

There is a principle which may be regarded as legal as well as moral, which is, that, as private power over the welfare of others increases, public responsibility for the welfare of others also increases as a legal and enforceable obligation. It is now well recognized that the conduct of the great industries in a modern nation involves such great power over the national welfare that the managers of those industries have a public responsibility for the national welfare represented by

163

an increasing number of legal obligations. Among these are a great number and complexity of obligations to their employees.

In the same way, it must be recognized that the labor organizations in the great industries of the country have such vast power over the welfare of those industries, and hence over the public welfare, that they should likewise be subject to legal obligations to fulfill that public responsibility. In these circumstances, the conduct of labor relations as a form of civil warfare becomes as vicious and antiquated as the practice of dueling.

Centuries ago civilized men began establishing courts to settle all disputes, even of the most personal character, by a peaceful administration of justice instead of by trial by combat. Only gangsters, outlaws, and crazy people today resort to guns and fists to decide their business disagreements. In practically all social and business relations (except in the lunacy of labor relations) good citizens either use peaceful pressures or apply to the courts to adjust their conflicting interests.

Why do we still attempt to settle big and little disputes between employers and employes by force and violence? Why do workers go on strike, depriving themselves of wages they need, injuring the employers who provide them with work, and often imposing great hardship on an innocent public? Why do employers and employees waste enormous amounts of money and energy preparing for warfare and waging wars against each other?

Why do we, here in the United States, tolerate the waging of civil warfare as the means of settling industrial disputes, although we have full power to enact and enforce laws forbidding such warfare and providing the means for peaceful settlement of all industrial conflicts? Why is it that even in wartime we not only refuse to draft men to work for their country, but we actually legalize and support organizations that prevent men from working?

The answer is that we have been fed a mental poison for years which is responsible for the prevailing lunacy of our labor relations. That poison is that there is an irreconcilable conflict between the interests of employers and employees. Yet our whole history shows that there is a community of interest between employers and employees which is much more important to both of them than their competitive interest in sharing the rewards of their common effort.

First, they must work together to produce something of value to someone else. No one can do this job for them and their community of interest lies in producing and selling goods and services that others want and can buy. They are their own best judges of the fair conditions of their joint work and the fair sharing of its rewards. But, if self-interest blinds them to the point where they cannot agree, surely here is the obvious place to bring in the objective judgment of an impartial arbitrator. But a public arbitrator can only decide a simple dispute as a temporary action; he cannot tell employers and employees how to work together and make a success of their joint undertaking. Politicians are not trained or equipped to plan and manage business enterprises.

Yet, strange to say, those who shrink from the idea of calling in a public arbitrator to decide a particular disagreement between experienced management and experienced labor are the very ones who propose as an alternative the socialization of industry. In other words, they propose to substitute for the operation of industry by experienced management and experienced labor an ultimate control by inexperienced, unqualified politicians!

As we see our political economy sliding down from the uplands of a free economy into the morasses of state socialism, we may well ask ourselves why we tolerate the constant disruption of industry by strikes;

why we do not try for once in our economic history to insist upon the peaceful cooperation of management and labor.

The legal principle to be applied is a simple one. Labor relations, like all other social relations, should be based on voluntary agreement. If parties in association cannot agree, and the public is concerned in their disagreement, public tribunals should be available to settle their dispute temporarily for them. If they are unwilling to accept this public judgment, they may cease peacefully to have relations with each other. The one thing they should not be permitted legally to do is to resort to violence and coercion to force their will upon others—to deny the civil rights of individuals and to inflict injuries on opponents and on the public.

We should not tolerate the increasing menace of industrial warfare that is today simply a legalized form of civil warfare. A rule of law to preserve peace and to establish justice should prove to be as fruitful of human happiness in labor relations as it has been proved to be in all other human relations.

15

In Conclusion

THE FIRST essential in dealing with the evils that arise from labor union monopolies is to recognize that the monopolies exist. This little book has attempted to make that clear.

The second essential is to understand that it is the exercise of monopolistic powers that perpetuates union evils and makes their correction so difficult. Perhaps this book may make a contribution to such an understanding.

The third essential is to realize that any monopoly power is destructive of a free economy and the political-economic freedom of a free society. It has been a significant error of many true liberals to assume that a labor union monopoly might be beneficent. It has been an effort of this book to expose that error.

In conclusion it seems worth while to retrace our

steps and to call attention to the unwisdom of all the steps taken by the federal government to legalize and encourage the creation and exercise of monopoly powers by labor unions. This began in the Clayton Act of 1914, which in itself sought reasonably to extend relief to labor organizations from unfair and often partisan interpretations of existing laws. A labor union could easily be found to be a combination in restraint of trade, although designed and operated only as a method of reasonable cooperation among many persons to advance their common interests.

It was recognized, however, that all unions and all union activities could not be given a wholesale immunity from anti-monopoly laws, because unions might easily become the means of nullifying all these laws. So the Clayton Act carefully provided only an immunity from anti-trust prosecution for organizations "lawfully" carrying out their "legitimate objects." Obviously, the authors of the Clayton Act and the Congressmen who voted for it had no expectation that the Supreme Court would hold that a union engaged in a sit-down strike was "lawfully" carrying out its objects. Nor was there an expectation that the Court would hold that writing contracts to monopolize the sale of electrical goods in New York City was a "legitimate object" of union activity.

Yet we have seen that the Supreme Court, combining later laws with the Clayton Act, has established such sweeping immunities for labor union monopolists.

It would need very little legislation, very simply worded, to restore the original Clayton Act limitations. For the benefit of a Supreme Court majority which overrules the dictionary as well as itself, the word "lawfully" could be defined so that unlawful conduct would not be immunized. Careful definitions could be written in the law explaining what are "legitimate objects" of union activity. Thus a majority instead of a minority of the Supreme Court might be induced to hold that violations of anti-trust laws and monopolistic contracts clearly in restraint of trade are not "legitimate objects" for a labor union to pursue.

In answer to official requests the writer has spelled out for Congress definitions that might be added to the law so as to make it more comprehensible to the Supreme Court. Here are two such definitions:*

"*First definition:* The 'legitimate objects' of labor organizations are defined to include the organization

---

* As revised for an article in *Human Events,* September 3, 1955.

and concerted activities of employees in protecting and promoting their interests in reasonable wages and working conditions, by any peaceful and lawful means, but shall not include the creation and exercise of such monopolistic controls over industry, trade or commerce among the several States, or with foreign nations, as to limit substantially competition in prices or quality of products or services, either nationally or within a local marketing area; and shall not include the making of agreements with employers providing that union membership shall be a condition of employment, whenever or wherever the consequence of such agreements shall be to threaten to give or shall give to a labor organization a monopolistic control over employments in an entire industry within the United States, or within one of the several States.

"Second definition: 'Lawfully carrying out the legitimate objects' of labor organizations is hereby defined to include any activities of a peaceful, orderly character which are not forbidden by any law of the United States or of the locality within which they are carired on, but shall not include any uses of fraud, force, violence or intimidation, or any conspiracy to violate or to prevent enforcement of any law of the United States or of one of the several States."

My first definition is intended to eliminate from

171

the legitimate objects of the labor organization the uniform negotiation of contracts which have the inevitable effect of substantially limiting competition "either nationally or within a local marketing area." It also excludes from a legitimate object the making of closed shop or union shop agreements which give a labor union a monopolistic control over employments.

The second definition is intended to carry out the vigorous dissents in the Supreme Court against a construction of federal law which leaves the government helpless to prevent the use of fraud, force, and violence as a deliberate policy of concerted action.

To restore the power of judicial enforcement of the anti-trust laws against labor unions, there should be added to the foregoing definitions a provision to the effect that the jurisdiction of any court of the United States to issue an injunction against a labor organization or its members who are found engaged in conduct which is not "lawfully carrying out the legitimate objects" of such an organization, shall not be restricted by the Clayton Act or the Norris-LaGuardia Act.

Even with "lawfully" and "legitimate" defined for an apparently illiterate judiciary there would still be the possibility of a long series of confusing decisions and opinions which would be troublesome alike to public officials and to labor unions. So it might be well to have legislation somewhat along the lines suggested in a previous chapter to limit industry-wide contract-making precisely and sufficiently to prevent it from being the means of establishing uniform standards of wages and working conditions of a monopolistic character.

Of course, the mere existence of a labor organization with over a hundred thousand members carries with it a financial, economic, and political power that threatens monopolistic controls of industry. On the other hand, the concentration of money and employment power in huge corporate enterprises offers the same threat. If size is not to be a measure of legality in business management it should not be made a measure in labor management.

It does seem, however, that the managers of union labor should be restricted to a law-abiding use of money and man power. They should not be free to attack physically and to terrorize either employers or employees who do not yield submissively to the coercion of a strike. If economic violence is to be left the final arbiter in labor relations, at least it should not be supported by legalized or legally tolerated, physical violence and intimidation.

There are many reasons for one to prefer state laws and state enforcement to eliminate the brutalities and lawlessness of strike violence. Such violence should be corrected, as other crimes are, primarily by local law-making and administration. Certainly the federal government should not "preempt" this field so as to exclude state action. But there are many ways and places where federal law could helpfully supplement —but not be substituted for—state law. The federal government already deals with such a vast field of labor relations, by virtue of Supreme Court expansion of the commerce clause, that it should no longer be possible for a federal court to avoid meeting the issue of the lawless conduct of a strike in a case within federal jurisdiction.

What is most needed at the present time is not the drafting of a lot of laws that will curb the economic and physical violence of labor union activities. What is most needed, and first needed, is an education of the so-called intellectual stratum of American life to a clear-eyed comprehension of the grave menace to our free economy and our free government in the unchecked growth and continuous spread of labor union monopolies.

Part of the monopoly power of labor unions arises from favoritism in legislation; part, from an unwarranted extension of this favoritism by Supreme Court interpretations; and part, from the timidity, unwillingness, or incapacity of local police officers to enforce the criminal law as it is applied to every other individual or organized violence except that occurring in a strike.

These evils will not be remedied until an overwhelming majority of free citizens realize that labor's economic monopoly and political power are preparing the way for communism far more effectively than the communists themselves. It is natural that union propaganda still portrays the unions as weak, defensive organizations of helpless wage earners who are forced to wage a continuing struggle against the ever-threatening oppression of great aggregations of heartless capital. As a matter of fact, the unions are powerful, aggressive organizations that are engaged in a continuing warfare against the maintenance of a free competitive economy. Unless this civil warfare is stopped and peaceful competition is substituted for monopolistic coercion in labor relations, a socialized economy and a socialist labor government are inevitable. This, unhappily, is not a remote prospect but one that is rapidly developing.